The Marshall Plan
for China

L. to R.: Paul G. Hoffman; Chiang Kai-shek, President of China; Li Tsung-jen, Vice-President of China; J. Leighton Stuart, American Ambassador to China.   *Griffin Papers. Hoover Institution on War, Revolution and Peace*

THE MARSHALL PLAN
FOR CHINA
Economic Cooperation
Administration
1948-1949

Grace M. Hawes

Schenkman Publishing Company, Inc.
Cambridge, Massachusetts

To:
John,
Clarence and Mabel
Elizabeth, John D., Mark and Amy.

Copyright © 1977

Schenkman Publishing Company, Inc.
3 Mt. Auburn Place
Cambridge, Massachusetts 02138

Library of Congress Cataloging in Publication Data

Hawes, Grace M.
    The Marshall Plan for China

    Includes bibliographical references.

    1. Economic assistance, American — China.
2. China — Economic conditions — 1912-1949.
3. United States. Economic Cooperation Administration. I.Title.

HC427.8.H39   338.91'51'073   76-40300
ISBN 0-87073-373-7

Printed in the United States of America

CONTENTS

MAPS

ACKNOWLEDGMENTS

It is with pleasure that I take this opportunity to thank some of the people who have helped me, listened to me, read the manuscript for me, and in many other ways made a difference to my progress on the book and to my life in general.

A very special thank you goes to my dear friend, Louisa M. Kilgroe, who first got me interested in China and who shared every exhilarating moment of my research.

Many people at San Jose State University helped me in the years I was a student there and to all of them I am deeply indebted. Irma Eichhorn literally taught us how to do research in one intense semester. If I have halfway lived up to her high standards, I will be pleased. Dr. David W. Eakins' classes gave me a new perspective on recent American history; a perspective which I hope and believe has brought me closer to understanding the period about which I write. Dr. Gerald E. Wheeler, Chairman of the History Department, and Dr. Claude A. Buss, Emeritus Professor of History from Stanford who now teaches at San Jose, read and commented on the manuscript several times. I deeply appreciate their willingness to give up their valuable time for me, and I especially want to thank them for believing in my work. This book would not exist without their encouragement.

The staff of the Hoover Institution Archives was unfailingly friendly and helpful and I want them to know how much I appreciate their assistance. I am especially beholden to Dr. Franz Lassner for allowing me to be the first researcher in Roger D. Lapham's papers. And to Crone Kernke and Ronald Bulatoff, I want to express my sincerest thanks.

I had the good fortune to be the first researcher in another set of papers, and to their owner, R. Allen Griffin, I owe an enormous debt of gratitude. He loaned me his papers, and talked to me at length about the China Mission. Both the papers and the interviews gave me insights into the Economic Cooperation Administration and American policy in China that I could have obtained in no other way.

Loving thanks to my daughters, Elizabeth and Amy, who have recently become proficient proofreaders.

To all of you, with warmest regards and sincerest gratitude, I dedicate this book.

Grace M. Hawes
Saratoga, California

Introduction

After World War II, the United States stepped into a new role as a powerful international leader determined to bring into being an era of peace and stability. The ordered world America envisioned, however, soon erupted with problems. One of the first areas of concern was China where, in the fall of 1945, the civil war broke out anew between Chiang Kai-shek's Nationalists and Mao Tse-tung's Communists. Hoping to stabilize the situation with a coalition government, President Harry S. Truman sent a renowned emissary to arbitrate, General of the Army George C. Marshall. When the General's mission failed in early 1947, United States policy makers, with Marshall as the new Secretary of State, tried to back away from active involvement in China and tried to re-assess American interests and goals. As steps toward disengagement from the Nationalists, the administration withdrew aid and placed an embargo on arms shipments. Concomitantly, as the Cold War with Russia intensified throughout 1947, Washington decided to place first priority on Europe. Just as in World War II, when policy makers concluded that the United States did not have the strength to fight a two-front war simultaneously, now America's leaders concluded that the national interest would be best served by concentrating on meeting the challenge in Europe first.

The Truman Doctrine and the Marshall Plan outlined the administration's methods for meeting the European crisis. Only when these programs for Europe were threatened with defeat by administration critics in Congress did the President and the policy makers agree to also back an aid program for China. Congress codified part of the "second front" program as the China Aid Act of 1948. To carry out the program on both continents the legislation formed a new agency called the Economic Cooperation Administration. ECA, as it came to be known, lasted a little less than a year on mainland China. Created on April 2, 1948, the mission did not begin its work until June; the following April when the Chinese Communists crossed the Yangtze into southern China, ECA operations were all but over. A few months after its demise, eminent historian and scholar, Dr. Dorothy Borg, wrote of the mission, "Since 1948, much of the active China policy of the United States has been channeled into the operations of the Economic Cooperation Administration." [1]

1

During the time when it constituted "much of the active China policy," ECA set up and administered three aid programs — a commodities program which acquired and distributed food, petroleum products, cotton, and fertilizer primarily to seven major port cities, an industrial reconstruction program designed to help key Chinese industries, and a rural reconstruction program. Military aid was also provided under the China Aid Act, and, although ECA officials were not in charge of its dispersal, they occasionally recommended areas where they felt military supplies were most needed and would be most effectively used.

In Washington their recommendations received a somewhat less than enthusiastic response, but throughout the length of the mission, ECA officials in China not only continued to make suggestions on the distribution of military aid, but also gave advice on the use of other aid, and on China policy in general. The results of their exhortations, the effectiveness of the aid programs, and the overall outcome of ECA as a major effort of American China policy in 1948-49 are the subjects to which this book is addressed.

[1] Dorothy Borg, "ECA and US Policy in China," *Far Eastern Survey,* XVIII (August 24, 1949), 197.

The Marshall Mission

After World War I, American policy makers began to recognize that the growing power of Japan posed a threat to United States interests in the Pacific. Casting about for a viable means of offsetting this menace they decided that a "strong, united, democratic" China as a friend and ally in the Far East would be one way to maintain a balance of power. Throughout the 1920's and 1930's, however, America backed up this policy with little more than moral and rhetorical support.

When war ultimately broke out between the United States and Japan in 1941, America's China policy assumed more tangible form and economic and military aid began to flow to Chiang Kai-shek. Concomitantly, American leaders began to act as if China were an important international power, one of the "Big Four." Despite the reluctance of his powerful ally, Winston Churchill,* President Franklin D. Roosevelt persisted in including China in wartime agreements between the United States, Britain and the Soviet Union. In Moscow on October 30, 1943, these countries signed an agreement which gave China the right "to participate jointly with the other great powers in the prosecution of the war, the organization of the peace, and the establishment of machinery for post-war international cooperation."[1] Chinese representatives attended other wartime conferences and, in 1945, participated in United Nations' organization meetings. The United Nations Charter that came out of these meetings gave China a permanent seat on the Security Council.[2]

---

* In a letter to Stanley K. Hornbeck, a State Department Political Adviser, dated August 7, 1944, from British Ambassador to Portugal, Ashley Clarke, Churchill's "reluctance to acknowledge China as a great power" was discussed. In the letter Clarke made a number of interesting observations. "It would be quite unsafe to attempt to interpret his thought on this subject in detail. But we are on firm ground in asserting that Mr. Churchill is a great realist and that he is accustomed to look at things as they are rather than as they might well become. He would not deny that the Chinese are a great nation and that China is a very big country. Nor have I ever seen or heard any statement by him to the effect that China was not potentially a great power or that her development into one of the great powers of Asia was in any way something which we should not wish to assist.

3

In spite of American support, the country's international eminence
in the postwar world could not, in fact, be upheld indefinitely. China's
economic and political problems resurfaced almost immediately and
revealed the existence of deep internal instability. By the fall of 1945
fighting had again broken out between the Nationalists led by Chiang
Kai-shek and the Communists led by Mao Tse-tung. This struggle over
which party was to rule the country had broken into warfare intermit-
tently since the 1920's and although they had formed a united front
against the Japanese, their uneasy alliance disintegrated just weeks
after Japan was defeated.

The renewal of the civil war was a cause for concern in Washington
since China was still important to American plans. In a meeting on
December 8, 1945, Secretary of State James F. Byrnes commented that,
"a strong unified China" was needed as a counterbalance to Russian
interests in Manchuria and North China.[3] As Byrnes' statement indicated, policy aims for the Far East were unchanged; in the postwar
world, however, it was the Soviet Union, not Japan, whose power was to
be offset by Chinese strength.

As a first step toward the realization of American objectives, President Truman asked General George C. Marshall to represent him on a
special mission to try to bring the Nationalists and the Communists

---

"Historically Great Britain has always favoured a united China with a strong central
government because — if for no other less sordid reasons — internal disturbance has
always been bad for business, and we are a nation of shopkeepers. Moreover, China
herself has manifested in these latter years in a striking manner her growing national
consciousness and her determination with such help as she can get from outside to
develop into a strong, stable and modern country. Most people would say, I fancy, that
China will get that help whatever happens and will at least go far to achieving her
ambitions. So that the point at issue is not whether China is or is not going to develop into
a great power one day but whether there is virtue in the proposition that it is in the
interests of the United Nations (a) that there should be only one strong power 'some-
where in Asia' and (b) that this unique Asiatic strong power should be China.

"In the first place, when Japan has been defeated, is it not a *fact* that, measured by any
conceivable criterion and without any building up from anyone else and whether all the
allies agree or not, there will be one very strong Asiatic power in Asia with a prestige
greater than any other power in the world except the United States and the British
Commonwealth: namely Russia? So if there is only to be one strong power in Asia, there
you are." Stanley K. Hornbeck Papers, Hoover Institution on War, Revolution and
Peace, Stanford, California. (Box numbers which would ordinarily be included in a
citation from this huge collection have been eliminated herein. This research was done
when the Hornbeck Papers were under a preliminary filing system. Subsequent re-filing
has made the old numbers meaningless and for this reason they have not been cited.)

together and end the war. In his memoirs, the President discussed
some of the problems United States policy makers and Marshall encountered:

> We in America always think of China as a nation. But the truth is that in
> 1945 China was only a geographical expression. Not since the Manchu
> Empire broke up in 1911 had there been in China a central government
> with authority over all the land. This was the state of China when V-J Day
> came. Chaing Kai-shek's authority was confined to the southwest corner,
> with the rest of South China and East China occupied by the Japanese.
> North China was controlled by the Communists and Manchuria by the
> Russians.[4]

In these reflections, the President outlined the three policy choices
faced by his administration. First, total American pullout. This alternative was not considered seriously because there were more than three
million Japanese still in China. Of these, one million were military
personnel who might have gained control of the country if the forces of
the United States had pulled out. Second, unlimited aid in the form of
arms and American troops. This option was rejected, since the American public would not have supported any move to send or retain troops
anywhere overseas immediately after World War II. The third policy
choice was the only one that seemed feasible and the one the
administration chose to pursue. The American government would
give all help to Chiang Kai-shek "politically, economically, and within
limits, militarily." At the same time, however, the United States "could
not become involved in a fratricidal war in China."[5]

Implementation of this third choice started with the Marshall mission. On the eve of Marshall's departure, the President publicly announced the China policy of the United States. The civil war, Truman
pointed out, threatened "world stability and peace" and with the goal
of a "strong, united and democratic China" in mind, America hoped to
bring an end to hostilities and to help the warring factions form a
coalition. This was to be done primarily through the Nationalist regime, which was the "only legal government" and "the proper instrument to achieve the objective of a unified China." The "Chinese
themselves" should work out "the detailed steps necessary to the
achievement of political unity," because "China has a clear responsibility to the other United Nations to eliminate armed conflict within its
territory as constituting a threat to world stability and peace." If the
Chinese proved able to resolve their difficulties, the President prom-

ised that the United States would help "to rehabilitate the country, improve the agrarian and industrial economy, and establish a military organization capable of discharging China's national and international responsibilities."[6]

A former American ambassador to China felt this speech marked a fundamental and important change in the country's foreign policy. Nelson T. Johnson, in a letter to John K. Fairbank, wrote that he considered the statement:

> Unprecedented among State papers of the United States, unprecedented in that it was a justification of intervention in the internal affairs of another country in the "interest of peace." This statement introduced an entirely new doctrine which in the years to come will, I believe, be discussed and debated quite as thoroughly as the Monroe Doctrine or the Open Door Doctrine. This Doctrine of Intervention cuts across one of the fundamental principles that has guided American foreign policy since the days of Washington. Namely, the principle of non-involvement and non-intervention in the domestic affairs of other countries.[7]

Policy makers, however, were unaware of the far-reaching significance of the "Doctrine of Intervention." They realized neither the unprecedented quality of their moves nor the dichotomy in seeking a coalition government in China while supporting one faction in the civil war. Many years later, Dean Acheson, who had been Undersecretary of State at the time, admitted, "Few, if any of us, including Hurley, myself, the Secretary, General Marshall, and the President, realized that these admirable aims were mutually exclusive and separately unachievable."[8]

* * *

Given the task of carrying out this ambiguous policy, General Marshall left for China in December, 1945. He was perhaps the most respected man in the country and the most distinguished representative the President could have chosen. As United States Chief of Staff during World War II, he had been one of the most powerful men in the world. His wartime status had capped an Army career characterized by steady advancement since 1902 when he was commissioned a second lieutenant.

One phase of his career had been a tour of duty in China in the 1920's. According to Marshall's biographer, Robert Payne, the General had wanted to go to China because of his interest in Chinese art, history and language. During his stay, he tried to learn Chinese, organized a language course for officers and men of the regiment, and wrote a "series of simplified Chinese textbooks." [9] In a letter to General John Pershing, at this time, Marshall revealed his concern for the problems China presented to the world:

> How the Powers should deal with China is a question almost impossible to answer . . . there has been so much of bitter hatred in the hearts of these people and so much of important business interests involved, that a normal solution can never be found. It will be some form of evolution, and we can only hope that sufficient tact and wisdom will be displayed by foreigners to avoid violent phases during the trying period that is approaching. [10]

"Violent phases" were not to be averted, however, and twenty years later, Marshall's mission to China was involved in one of those phases. All the "tact and wisdom" he could muster were needed.*

There were three major goals in the General's plan of action: help establish a coalition government, form one army, and with the help of American aid, re-establish a sound economy. His initial successes were impressive. Less than three weeks after he arrived in China, the Nationalists and the Communists signed a truce, and shortly thereafter they agreed to merge their armies. [11] The cease-fire was signed on January 10, 1946, and on the same day the Political Consultative Conference convened. There were representatives from the Nationalists, the Communists, the Democratic League, the Youth party, as well as

---

* Mrs. Rose Page Wilson had been a friend of Marshall's since she met him in Washington in 1920 when she was a child. Of his mission to China, she wrote, "Yet, I think his acceptance of the China assignment was the hardest self-disciplinary act of his life. His first letter to me from China, written a few weeks after he had arrived, shocked me, not because he was unhappy and homesick, but because he admitted it. His letters during the war had frequently mentioned how busy he was, or how lonely his horseback rides were, or how weary he was then about the pressure of the terrible responsibilities he bore; but his observations of this sort had been made off-handedly, more as reasons for not writing sooner. His January letter from China was the first and only letter to me wherein Colonel Marshall (Mrs. Wilson had always called Marshall "Colonel," the rank he had when she met him) allowed himself to confess that he was downright miserable. He wrote that he left home with a minimum of preparation. Not only was his time short, but most of his days had been taken up by Congressional hearings. During his lunch hours, he had had to rush over to the White House or the State Department. Since his arrival in China, he had been 'intensely busy' every hour from nine to five, sometimes until midnight, and it looked as if the grinding pace would keep up for some time to come." Rose Page Wilson, *General Marshall Remembered* (Englewood Cliffs, N.J.: Prentice-Hall, 1968), pp. 313-14.

other unaligned delegates. In three weeks they agreed on the organization of a new coalition government, and, by the end of February, they had worked out a military agreement to integrate and reduce the size of the armies. The latter was especially important since they hoped to prevent partisan armies from again dividing the country into warring sections. After the agreements were signed, China seemed well on her way to unity and Marshall's mission seemed assured of success.

This amicable rapprochement was short-lived, however, for in a few weeks, fighting again broke out in Manchuria where the cease-fire failed to be effective.[12] Russian troops had remained in Manchuria after the war and their announcement that they would not leave until milder spring weather permitted troop movement caused both the United States and the Nationalists to suspect that the Russians might be lingering to give help to the Chinese Communists. Alarmed by this and aware of the growing differences between the Soviet Union and the United States, Chiang Kai-shek seemed determined to regain control of Manchuria with all haste. He believed he had the advantage militarily and could defeat the Communists. The subsequent Nationalist movements in North China in turn caused the Russians to suspect that Manchuria might indeed be an area of conflict between Soviet and American interests.[13]

In this international aura of mistrust, Marshall returned to China in April after a short trip to Washington. He found the successes of January had disappeared, and unfortunately for his work as mediator, as Theodore White and Annalee Jacoby observed:

> The Communists . . . were now convinced that America was in active league with the Kuomintang.* Despite Marshall's personal integrity, American ships continued to move government troops north to the battle zone of Manchuria; American experts and technicians arrived at Shanghai with every boat from the Pacific to strengthen the government's administration; American relief supplies, wretchedly maladministered by the government, created wealth for profiteers at the coast, while peasants starved in Communist territory.[14]

Alarmed by the help Chiang received from the United States, the Communists were further incensed by Washington's decision to send

---

* Kuomintang means National People's Party and is the same as the Nationalist Party. It is also called the KMT. To avoid confusion in this book, it will be referred to as the Nationalist Party or the Nationalists, except in direct quotes.

more American advisers to the Nationalists. This happened during the summer of 1946, midway in the Marshall mission. The President "directed the establishment of a small military advisory group in China"[15] to give advice to Chiang Kai-shek's troops. The Communists objected to help being sent to their enemies and to American interference in China's internal affairs. In a statement issued on July 5, 1946, they asked the United States "to stop fostering civil war, to stop sending military supplies and military advisers, and to withdraw immediately all military forces from China."[16]

The Communists' verbal assaults on American policy in general and Marshall's efforts in particular were not without foundation nor were they surprising under the circumstances. Criticism from another group, however, was unexpected. A conservative faction in Chiang Kai-shek's party accused the United States of pursuing an economic policy detrimental to China's progress. They said American business interests, who favored their own goods over Chinese goods, damaged the country's economy. They further charged that General Marshall and those who agreed with him among the Nationalists undermined the best interests of the government by showing undue restraint in dealing with the Communists. The conservatives wanted to launch an all-out campaign to rid the country of Mao and his followers.[17] They wanted no further attempts at coalition government.

Apparently Generalissimo Chiang agreed with his right-wing supporters, for he and the Communists continued to try to solve their differences on the battlefield. In later testimony Dean Acheson discussed the overriding importance both sides placed on a military solution and the debilitating effect this had on negotiations.[18] "Either the Communists would attack the Nationalists or the Nationalists would attack the Communists, and in that way this situation became worse and worse; and General Marshall's efforts were unable to deal with it." Negotiations, meanwhile, "got into more and more confusion and trouble."[19]

Unable to cope satisfactorily with the revolutionary forces or to mediate their differences, Marshall left China in January, 1947. He had not been able to fulfill the goals American policy had set for him: the coalition government had not materialized, the armies had not been integrated, and therefore, the United States would not give the massive assistance needed to achieve economic stability. The old

American dream of China as a united, democratic, stable ally in the Far East had not come true, and Marshall left China disgusted with both the Nationalists and the Communists.

John Robinson Beal, who was an American press adviser to the Nationalists, recalled a conversation he had with the General just before the mission ended. Marshall said it was the Nationalists' fault they were "in this hole. They had told him in June it would take them only two months to clear the Communists out of northern Kiangsu and they weren't out yet." The General said he warned the Nationalists that "their military miscalculations had created a financial vacuum into which they were expecting the U.S. to pour taxpayers' money, and he refused to recommend that." [20] Marshall's complaint that the Nationalists ignored his military counsel was brought up later in testimony by Dean Acheson:

> General Marshall repeatedly pointed out to the Government that . . . it
> . . . was over extending itself militarily and politically, since it neither had
> sufficient troops to garrison this whole area nor . . . sufficient adminis-
> trators to administer the areas that it was taking over. [21]

Early in January, 1947, the General left China. In his parting statement, he took the opportunity to rebut accusations made against him and to place the responsibility for the failure of his mission where he felt it rightly belonged, on the Chinese. He singled out the conservative members of the Nationalist party, a "dominant group of reactionaries," who resisted "almost every effort I have made to influence the formation of a genuine coalition government."

The Communists bore a large share of the responsibility for thwarting his mission as well. The General concluded:

> Between this dominant reactionary group in the Government and the
> irreconcilable Communists, who, I must state, did not so appear last
> February, lies the problem of how peace and well-being are to be brought
> to the long-suffering and presently inarticulate mass of the people of
> China.

Since the "greatest obstacle to peace" had been the "almost overwhelming suspicion with which the Chinese Communist Party and the Kuomintang regard each other," Marshall felt:

> The salvation of the situation, as I see it, would be the assumption of
> leadership by the liberals in the Government and in the minority parties,

a splendid group of men, but who as yet lack the political power to exercise a controlling influence. Successful action on their part under the leadership of Generalissimo Chiang Kai-shek would, I believe, lead to unity through good government.[22]

Marshall's advice seemed to suggest the formation of a coalition government by the "liberal elements" in both parties. This was more unrealistic in January, 1947, than it had been in 1946. The "liberal elements" did not control the armies, and, as one historian observed, both parties "counted their support not in votes but in divisions. Political power in China since the fall of the Manchu Empire was indentical with military power; a party without an army could not exist."[23] Marshall's recommendations, therefore, went unheeded.

On his return to Washington, the General became the new Secretary of State. Influenced by his experience in China he seemed determined to detach the United States from further involvement or responsibility for events there. Total detachment from China's problems, however, proved to be impossible, and, although Marshall criticized the Nationalists for being "weak, shifty, unreliable and insincere," American supplies continued to go to Chiang Kai-shek and American agreements remained in force.[24]

In some measure this ambivalence on the part of policy makers was due to the difficulty of fitting China into their assessment of the world situation; a view which increasingly interpreted all international events as though they were related to the growing conflict between the two superpowers. The Russians carefully emphasized that they recognized Chiang Kai-shek, and they did not overtly support the Chinese Communists. For this reason, as historian Walter Lafeber pointed out, "American officials were hard put to place the growing disaster in China within the standard Cold War context."[25]

Firmly within the context, however, were Soviet actions in Europe. In an important policy decision early in 1947, American leaders determined that the threat to Europe had to be met. They concluded that by concentrating their efforts where there were ancient ties, an industrial base, and a great power potential, the national interests of the United States would be best served. At the same time, China dropped "down the list of American diplomatic priorities."[26] In the Cold War, China was again a secondary theatre. The World War II strategy of holding in the Pacific while taking the offensive in Europe was being repeated.

Chapter 1 Footnotes

[1] *The China White Paper*, August 1949 (2 vols; Stanford, California: Stanford University Press, 1967), I, 37. Originally issued as *United States Relations with China, with Special Reference to the Period 1944-1949*. Hereinafter cited as *China White Paper*.

[2] *Ibid*.

[3] Walter Millis (ed.), *The Forestall Diaries* (New York: The Viking Press, 1951), p. 113.

[4] Harry S. Truman, *Memoirs*, Vol. II: *Years of Trial and Hope, 1946-1952* (New York: Signet Book, 1956), p. 80.

[5] *Ibid*., p. 82. Truman's views of China and of United States China policy immediately after World War II are to be found on pp. 80-114.

[6] *China White Paper*, II. The full text of the President's statement may be found on pp. 607-609.

[7] Stanley K. Hornbeck Papers, Hoover Institution on War, Revolution and Peace, Stanford, California. This is an excerpt from a letter to John K. Fairbank dated August 4, 1948. The copy in Hornbeck's papers is addressed to Fairbank and is a twenty-six page critique of his recently published book *The United States and China*.

[8] Dean Acheson, *Present at the Creation: My Years in the State Department* (New York: W. W. Norton & Company, 1969), p. 135.

[9] Robert Payne, *The Marshall Story: A Biography of General George C. Marshall* (New York: Prentice-Hall, Inc., 1951), p. 103.

[10] *Ibid*., p. 104.

[11] *Ibid*., p. 260.

[12] John K. Fairbank, *The United States and China* (New York: The Viking Press, 1948), p. 267.

[13] O. Edmund Clubb, *Twentieth Century China* (New York: Columbia University Press, 1964), p. 265.

[14] Theordore H. White and Annalee Jacoby, *Thunder Out of China* (New York: William Sloane Associates, Inc., 1946), p. 295.

[15] *China White Paper*, I, 170.

[16] Clubb, *Twentieth Century China*, p. 277.

[17] *China White Paper*, I, 170.

[18] C. P. Fitzgerald, *The Birth of Communist China* (Baltimore, Maryland: Penguin Books, 1964), p. 96.

[19] U. S. Congress. Senate, Hearings before the Committee on Armed Services and the Committee on Foreign Relations, 82nd Cong. 1st Sess., *Military Situation in the Far East* (5 vols.; Washington, 1951), III, 1851. Hereinafter cited as *Military Situation in the Far East*.

[20] John Robinson Beal, *Marshall in China* (Toronto: Doubleday Canada Limited, 1970), p. 4.

[21] *Military Situation in the Far East*, III, 1852. See also Rose Page Wilson, *General Marshall Remembered* (Englewood Cliffs, N.J.: Prentice-Hall, 1968), p. 377 for a conversation with the General she recalled having on the subject of Chiang Kai-shek as China's leader and of his disregard for Marshall's advice.

[22] *China White Paper*, II, Marshall's statement may be found on pp. 686-689.

[23] Fitzgerald, *The Birth of Communist China*, p. 95.

[24] *Ibid*., p. 102.

[25] Walter Lafeber, *America, Russia, and the Cold War 1945-1966* (New York: John Wiley and Sons, Inc., 1967), p. 27.

[26] *Ibid*.

The China Aid Act of 1948

Throughout 1947 policy makers were influenced by three major areas of concern as they attempted to formulate an effective China policy. First, American officials recognized the growing threat to United States leadership and hegemony from the Soviet Union, especially in Europe. The desire to "contain" communism became the basis for foreign policy throughout this period. Second, the administration was troubled by the complexity of the situation in China where the United States backed a regime it recognized as corrupt and weak, yet for which there seemed no viable alternative. The other strong party was Communist and American officials felt they could hardly support the Chinese Communists while resisting their ideology elsewhere in the world. This situation became even more difficult to deal with as the military threat of the Communist armies grew. Third, American leaders had to consider their need for support within their own country. Increasingly during 1947, administration critics grew more vociferous and antagonistic, especially a group in Congress which came to be known as the China bloc. They demanded help for Chiang Kai-shek and insisted that American interests were as vital in Asia as in Europe. Although they were willing to support the administration's foreign policy programs, they were determined to obtain aid for China as well. If not, they threatened to oppose all foreign aid.

Confronted with this adamant and powerful opposition and determined to ensure passage of legislation for the European Recovery Program, the Truman administration made several strategic concessions to the China bloc. According to the reminiscences of then Under Secretary of State Dean G. Acheson, the plans for Europe were safeguarded by taking the following actions to placate the critics:

> On May 26, 1947, the embargo on shipment of munitions to China was lifted. From April to September, as the Marines withdrew from north China, they "abandoned" to the Nationalist forces sixty-five hundred tons of ammunition. In July General Wedemeyer was sent on a fact-finding mission to China. In September John Carter Vincent was relieved as Chief of the Office of Far Eastern Affairs — being succeeded by Walton Butterworth — and sent to Switzerland as Minister, both to appease Republican critics and to remove him from the direct path of Republican vengeance. In 1948 the Administration agreed to a China Aid Act even larger than that finally enacted.[1]

13

The pressure exerted on the administration by the China bloc prevented the complete end to American involvement. On the other hand, the administration's attitude prevented a substantive American commitment. Again in 1947, as they had in 1945, the policy alternatives brought forth the same conclusion: neither total pullout nor total commitment was possible. Once more the only feasible choice seemed to be some form of aid to Chiang Kai-shek.

Administration spokesmen, though they supported the China aid proposals in their testimony before Congressional committees and in public statements, expressed few illusions about effecting major changes in the situation in China. Late in 1947, in a statement to the House Committee on Foreign Affairs, Marshall said the purpose of additional aid was "to see what can be done toward a stay of execution in the deterioration of their monetary situation so as to give them a chance, with . . . very energetic action on their part, to take some measure toward restoring the financial situation." [2]

The planning for the "stay of execution" went on throughout the winter and on February 18, 1948, the President presented a request for legislation to Congress. In spite of the growing controversy over China policy and further aid, the legislation requested by the President was almost assured of passage.

According to one political analyst, Robert A. Dahl, members of Congress look to three areas for leadership on foreign affairs: the President, Committee Chairmen and Congressional bellwethers. The legislative history of the China Aid Act of 1948 reveals that it had the support of all three. [3] The President, though neither enthusiatic about aid nor convinced of its efficacy, requested passage, therefore putting his administration's power and influence at least tacitly behind the bill. The important Committee Chairmen also favored aid to China. The two most influential were Arthur Vandenberg, Chairman of the Senate Foreign Relations Committee and Charles Eaton, Chairman of the House Committee on Foreign Affairs. Congressional bellwethers supported the legislation as well.

According to Dahl, the bellwether

> In foreign affairs, . . . is one who has somehow earned a reputation for knowledge and understanding of some international problem or area; he is, in a word, one whom his colleagues regard as relatively more "expert" than they, and yet sufficiently akin to them to be trustworthy. In

the Eighty-first Congress, one could point to Representative Walter Judd, of Minnesota, who had been a medical missionary and hospital superintendent in China for ten years; or Mike Mansfield, of Montana, who had been stationed in the Orient with the Marines and later taught Latin American and Far Eastern history in Montana State University.[4]

Although the President's endorsement is usually the most important influence for the passage of foreign policy legislation, in this case it seems that the influence of the chairmen, especially Vandenberg, and the bellwethers, especially Judd, was equally as vital. Vandenberg rallied the support of the Senate and Judd the support of the House.

INFLUENCE OF THE ADMINISTRATION FOR CHINA AID

The message the President sent Congress on February 19, 1948, explained that China had special problems which were almost impossible to solve because of the war and the state of the economy. The purpose of American aid, therefore, was to provide "a respite from rapid economic deterioration," so the Nationalist government could "move to establish more stable economic conditions." Without American help, the President felt the Chinese would be unlikely to stabilize conditions. Truman admitted the aid was no panacea for China's problems, but felt that "the achievement of even this limited objective is of such importance as to justify the proposed program of aid."[5]

Two days after the President sent his aid message to Congress, Secretary of State Marshall appeared before an executive session of the Committees on Foreign Affairs and Foreign Relations. In his statement, Marshall also expressed few illusions about the effectiveness of aid on the problems China faced. Marshall stated that since 1945, "virtually every American authority" agreed that the Nationalists could not win a military victory over the Communists for several reasons: China's terrain lent itself to the success of the guerrilla tactics used by the Communist armies; the Nationalist army's low morale, often caused by the "conspicuous ineptitude and widespread corruption among the higher leaders," contributed to its ineffectiveness; and the Communists had been successful in destroying the economy of China, which Marshall declared had been one of their avowed objectives. The Communists had also been able to identify "their movement with the popular demand for change" in China. The Secretary said he knew of many young educated Chinese who had chosen the Communist party as the only available alternative to the corruption and ineffectiveness of the Nationalists. The Nationalist government was "not only weak, but" lacked "self-discipline and inspiration," and Marshall felt it unlikely that "these conditions can be basically corrected by foreign aid." As evidence of this, the Secretary stated, American aid had been substantial since World War II and had included the equiping and training of thirty-nine divisions, military lend-lease of more than $700,000,000, a gift of ninety-seven naval craft, a United States military advisory group, surplus munitions, and a good deal more; all of which added up to "$1,432,000,000, at least half of which" had been "military assistance."

In spite of this tremendous amount of aid, the situation in China had not improved economically and the Nationalists had not been able to win the war against the Communists. Marshall hoped that they would realize that henceforth they would have to rely on themselves if they were to prove successful. Americans, on the other hand, who wanted to help the Chinese should be aware that the United States could overextend itself by trying to meet the Communist challenge wherever it presented itself around the globe. Under those circumstances, the initiative would always be in Communist hands and American efforts would be diffused and weakened. Marshall went on to suggest that perhaps the United States should not expect China to fill the role of stabilizing friend and ally in the Far East. He warned that China could not in the "foreseeable future" rise to be a world power. The "revolution" would have to be ended before the country could be stable, and a lack of "raw materials and industrial resources" made it unlikely that China could become a "first-class military power." The "more vital regions" of the world (meaning Europe) should receive first priority in American efforts.

The problems, then, as Marshall outlined them, were to provide some form of aid to China without encouraging the Chinese to become too dependent on the United States and without overextending America's global efforts. Marshall admitted that since the end of his mission to China, he had "struggled and puzzled over the situation continuously." [6]

It is unlikely that Marshall or the President considered the China Aid Act the answer to hours of struggling with the problem, but in his statement to the committees, the Secretary said that he hoped the aid would:

Assist in arresting the accelerating trend of economic deterioration to provide the Chinese Government with a further opportunity to lay the groundwork for stabilizing the situation. In these circumstances, I consider that this program of economic assistance, proposed with full recognition of all the unfavorable factors in the situation, is warranted by American interests.[7]

The President's and Secretary's statements left no doubt that they held little hope that their "limited objectives" would be able to provide more than a "stay of execution," but even this lukewarm support proved enough when combined with the more enthusiastic backing of the committee chairmen and bellwethers.

INFLUENCE OF THE COMMITTEE CHAIRMEN ON CHINA AID

Arthur H. Vandenberg, Republican from Michigan, President Pro Tempore of the Senate, Chairman of the Foreign Relations Committee, foremost leader of bipartisan foreign policy, "strongly" supported the China Aid Act of 1948.[8] The Senator, "in spite of the increasingly fluid situation in China, . . . believed it desirable to continue our program of assistance to Chiang Kai-shek so long as such aid could be used effectively against Communism." [9] With this in mind, on March 30, 1948, Vandenberg presented bill S.2393 to the Senate. It was "a bill to promote the general welfare, national interest, and foreign policy of the United States by providing aid to China." The Senator stated the bill had been unanimously approved by the Committee on Foreign Relations, and urged his colleagues to make a quick decision.

The Senate Committee recommended an appropriation of $463,000,000; $363,000,000 for "carefully screened relief and rehabilitation under the applicable provisions of the Economic Cooperation Act of 1948, including the usual bilateral agreement with China." The other provision of $100,000,000 would be grated "on such terms the President may determine," . . . and could be used "at China's option for military purposes in the purchase of urgently needed military supplies."

Senator Vandenberg admitted that the situation in China was "touch and go" and that reforms were needed in the Nationalist government, "but reforms without survival would be a disillusioning mirage." The military grant, therefore, seemed necessary "in order to make economic aid effective." Vandenberg assured his fellow Senators that the grant for military aid did not imply American responsibility for the

war or the possibility that American troops would be sent to China. The
United States would continue to send advisers, but not troops. Vandenberg concluded his statement with the hope that:

> The Senate will find it wise and profitable to pass this bill with least
> possible delay so that a final conference report on this entire peace
> program may light another torch of liberty before this weekend wanes.[10]

Though he did not use the same kind of splendid rhetoric, the
Senator's counterpart, Congressman Charles A. Eaton, Chairman of
the Committee on Foreign Affairs, also lent his support to China aid.
Eaton, a New Jersey Republican who had been a member of Congress
for twenty-four years, was known as a "strong, 'internationalist.' "[11]
He supported aid to China and hoped to get prestigious and expert
support for the bill by having General Douglas MacArthur testify
before a committee meeting. MacArthur, in a telegram dated March 3,
1948, sent his regrets to Eaton and stated he could not leave his post in
Japan. The General pointed out that he was not an expert on China or
aware of the detailed planning of China policy. "China, as you perhaps
know, is a theater of United States Navy control, outside the scope of
my existing authority." MacArthur went on, however, to affirm "that a
free, independent, peaceful, and friendly China is of profound importance to the peace of the world and to the position of the United States.
It is the fundamental keystone to the Pacific arch." Policy makers
should try to keep this in mind and strive for a global point of view.
"Fragmentary decisions in disconnected sectors of the world will not
bring an integrated solution;" one "frontier" should not receive preferential treatment. MacArthur obviously did not agree with the
administration's European-oriented policy, but felt, on the contrary,
that "while availing ourselves of the potential to the east, to our
western horizon we must look" as well. MacArthur also emphasized the
need for a military solution in China, after which, he felt, "reform will
gradually take place."[12]

The General's telegram lent support to Chairman Eaton's favorable
views on China aid. Both committee chairmen, with the support of
MacArthur's expertise were joined in their endorsement of China aid
by the bellwethers in the House.

INFLUENCE OF THE BELLWETHERS ON CHINA AID

According to Robert Dahl, the expert or bellwether influence is not as great in "the highly individualistic Senate" as in the House, where "many members hopelessly out-distanced by the complexity of an issue pay special attention to the attitudes of certain members to whose judgment, . . . they defer." [13]

One of the experts in Congress to whom his colleagues looked for foreign policy advice was Representative Mike Mansfield of Montana. Mansfield had lived in China, had spent many years studying the country, and had taught Far Eastern history in college. In an interesting speech in the House on March 31, 1948, Mansfield revealed a point of view close to the administration's. He emphasized the importance of Europe to American interests, and admitted he had grave reservations about the efficacy of aid to China. Disagreeing with General MacArthur and others, Mansfield thought reforms in China should come before military considerations.

> Any American aid should be conditioned by adequate reforms instituted in fact, and not on paper, for the benefit of the Chinese people. This, in turn, will strengthen the Nationalist Government, give the support needed to win the civil war, and thereby bring about the creation of a strong and united China.[14]

Mansfield's hesitant attitude on China aid contrasted sharply with the enthusiastic support of Congressman Walter H. Judd. As China expert, Judd proved to be the greater influence on his colleagues in the House, for he was undoubtedly one of the most fervid and tenacious anti-Communist, pro-Nationalist members of Congress. Judd had lived in China for many years where, in Fukien Province and later in Shansi Province, he headed missionary hospitals. Dr. Judd had stayed in China for five months after the Japanese captured the city where he lived. On his return to the United States in 1938, he made speeches in forty-six states in a two-year period "on the danger of Japanese expansion and the need of justice for China." [15] In 1942, he ran for Congress from Minnesota, and, as a Representative, he continued to espouse and support China's cause. During the war years when there was little opposition to China policy, Judd often put into the "Congressional Record his own observations on China's need for more aid and 'sympathetic' understanding, letters from his constituents supporting his views, and magazine and newspaper articles urging aid for China." [16]

When Judd visited China immediately after World War II, members of the North China Mission of the American Board tried to explain to the Congressman that conditions in China had changed since he had left in 1938, and attempted to let him know of the corruption of some of the Nationalists. One historian has noted that "They found Judd 'a tense and emotional man' who did all the talking while the rest of them listened — he made no converts there but he . . . built up a tremendous following for Chiang in the United States."[17]

Walter Judd traveled to China again during the fall of 1947 and came home determined to obtain more help for the Nationalists from Congress. On January 6, 1948, he spoke on a radio program called "The Town Meeting of the Air." The title of his talk was "What Should We Do In China Now?" He expressed his conviction that "without vigorous American aid the Chinese Government will almost certainly collapse." This "would bring the vast resources and manpower of China under the control of the ruthlessly efficient Communist government, subservient to the Soviet Union." America would have "to subsidize Japan and Korea" and send "troops to defend them, or else walk out on our promises to those peoples and abandon the whole western Pacific," even the Philippines. "It is over 50 years of splendid investment of American lives, efforts, and money in the Philippines that will go down the sewer." With "satellites and security all along her Asiatic frontiers," the Soviet Union could then "concentrate all her attention and efforts on Europe." The threat to the United States was obvious and aid to Chiang Kai-shek should be the first step in a plan to meet the potential danger. To those who questioned further aid to a regime that seemed less than effective, Judd admitted there were "bad elements" among the Nationalists, but, he pointed out, in a rather oblique rationale, that "recent history indicates all is not well in our own." He assured his listeners that American aid would not be wasted if "well handled," or "if China is free, she can and will move rapidly toward greater democracy and better government, as was proved during the period of peace from 1932-1937."* If the United States did not move to help the Nationalists, Judd warned, all of the gains made in World War II might be lost.

* The idea Judd discussed here is the subject of an article by Martin Bernal, "Was Chinese Communisim Inevitable?", *The New York Review of Books*, XV (December 3, 1970), 43-47. Bernal says, "This hypothesis that the K.M.T. were making progress, and might well have succeeded politically and economically had it not been for Japanese interference and invasion, has been widely accepted and used." On the contrary, Bernal concludes, "Before the Japanese intervened directly there was no steady trend to unity. All the evidence shows that even if the invasion had not taken place the internal and interna-

> If China is not to be free, then it would have been far better for her to be under Japan rather than under Russia. Not to aid her now may well mean that all the sacrifices in men and money in the Pacific during the war were useless; . . . because if we wind up with one imperialistic power, Russia, dominant in both Europe and Asia, then we will have less security than when we started.[18]

Judd's argument contributed to the passage of the China aid legislation in the House. The bill authorized $570,000,000 for aid over a fifteen-month period; $420,000,000 for economic aid and $150,000,000 for military aid. The military assistance was "to be supervised by an American military mission on the same basis as that which underlay provision of United States military aid in Greece."[19] Under this plan, America would have taken the "responsibility . . . for programming, procurement and delivery of military supplies . . . and for detailed supervision of their use in China, including operational advice to Chinese combat forces in the field."[20] Passage of the House bill would have led to greater United States involvement in China's civil war. A compromise with the Senate bill, however, changed the House military aid provision and averted the possibility of increased American involvement on the side of the Nationalists.

* * *

Before the aid bill passed, some members of Congress spoke in opposition. Although they were few in number and destined to be overruled, their views point up some of the basic questions foreign aid has been eliciting in all the years of its existence as an adjunct of American policy.

Opposition to China Aid

Senator James P. Kem, Republican of Missouri, represented the isolationist point of view. In the internationalist atmosphere of 1948 when foreign policy received bipartisan support, his was a minority opinion representing the judgment of a small group of conservatives. It is interesting to note that twenty years later the ideas Kem outlined

---

tional situation would never have allowed the Nationalists to unify China effectively. In view of the underlying social discontent and endemic civil war there is every reason to suppose that even if the Red Army had been defeated, Communists would have continued to exist and to have retained the potential for sudden expansion."

could be heard from a totally different part of the political spectrum — the liberal opponents of American foreign policy and the Viet Nam war.

The Senator, in the debate on China aid, first spoke of the "loan" to Greece and Turkey which he said "marked the initial phase of the so-called Truman doctrine to quarantine communism." Kem went on to outline his reasons for his opposition to foreign aid.

First, the United States had acted unilaterally, without consultation with the United Nations.

> Insofar as I am aware, there has been no action on our part to utilize the policing function of the United Nations in seeking a solution of the China problem. Did we not accept the United Nations as a means of world peace and security? Why, then, should the United States take unto itself the full responsibility of deciding how world peace should be maintained, when the problem had been and has been specifically assigned to the United Nations from the outset?

America, according to Kem, should use the money it planned for China aid to make the United Nations stronger.

Second, the plan for China, "although presented on a humanitarian basis," was essentially a "military program." Kem feared that military aid would soon lead to greater American involvement in the war. "Once we are committed, it is only a question of time till the American soldier will be called upon to follow the American dollar." The Senator could see very little difference in foreign aid wherever it was sent and sensed a pattern developing which would embroil America in problems all over the world. "Aid to Greece, aid to Turkey, aid to China have this in common. They are toll houses on the road to war."

Third, the United States could not buy goodwill around the world. In spite of aid America had already given, Kem concluded "We have never been able to convert any Communists to democratic concepts by the use of dollars." On the contrary, it seemed aid often had the opposite effect. "We still have not convinced many Europeans that Uncle Sam is not going on a wild spree of dollar imperialism with the Truman-Marshall plan." In China, aid had also won enemies for the United States. The Chinese resented American interference in their affairs and the growing unpopularity of the regime the United States supported would reap for America "only a lasting harvest of hatred." The Senator also pointed out the futility of affecting changes in China.

Aid to Europe had been poured down a "rat hole," but in China "we are confronted, . . . by no mere rat hole. It is rather a bottomless pit, or an abysmal morass." The proposed $450,000,000 in economic aid to China would amount to $1 per person, hardly enough to make a substantial change in the country. To Senator Kem, it seemed a "foolish use of the national wealth."

Fourth, America should concentrate on building its own economy. Problems in the United States should be considered first when appropriations were made for the use of national funds.

> It is perhaps proper for the Members of this body to concern themselves with conditions of fertility in the valley of the Yangtse, but for my part I am more concerned about the loss of fertility in the valleys of the Mississippi and the Missouri. It is perhaps proper for Members of this body to concern themselves with underprivileged children in Shanghai, Hong Kong, and Canton, but for my part . . . I am more concerned with underprivileged children in St. Louis and Kansas City, in New York and Chicago. It would be far better for us first to look after our own people, develop our own resources, and stabilize our own economy, instead of bankrupting the Nation, impoverishing our people, and inviting disaster.[21]

Kem's speech ended with his assertion that he would not vote for the aid bill. Senator William Langer, North Dakota Republican, shared Kem's opposition to foreign aid and in a lengthy speech stressed the needs of Americans. "Veterans, farmers, school teachers, Indians, and the underpriviledged of various classes have been suffering for a long time." [22] The two Senators agreed, American money should be used for the welfare of Americans.

Senator Wayne L. Morse of Oregon did not share his colleagues opposition to foreign aid in general but he did feel a certain inquietude about continued support for Chiang Kai-shek's government.

> I agree . . . that once China falls behind the iron curtain of communism there is no liberty at all. But if she becomes a completely Fascist state — and I am satisfied she is more Fascist today than democratic — there will be no personal liberty for the people of China. It will be lost to the same degree under fascism as it would be lost under communism.[23]

Morse's uneasiness about the character of the government of China and Kem's and Langer's opposition to aid did not forestall Congressional action, however, and three days after Morse made his speech, the China Aid Act of 1948 became law.

* * *

The differences between the House bill and the Senate bill were resolved in a conference committee and the act passed on April 2, 1948. The bill provided for two grants to China for economic aid and for military aid. Before funds were appropriated, economic aid was drastically reduced. The President had asked for $570,000,000; the House for $420,000,000; the Senate for $363,000,000. The amount requested after the meeting of the House/Senate conference committee was $338,000,000. Under the watchful eye of the economy-minded Congressman John Taber, Chairman of the House Appropriations Committee, the amount was further trimmed. The final appropriation was $275,000,000.*

The grant for military aid fared somewhat better. The amount finally appropriated for the special fund for military use was $125,000,000, exactly between the House request for $150,000,000 and the Senate request for $100,000,000. The provision in the House bill that would have placed greater responsibility on the United States for the war in China was removed, and the Senate proposal, that the grant be used by the Chinese government for military purposes, if it wished, was accepted.

The bill provided that an agreement on aid must be made with the Chinese government. Before the agreement was reached, however, and before the funds were appropriated, an advance from the Reconstruction Finance Corporation enabled the administering agency to start operation on part of the aid program.[24]

* * *

The Economic Cooperation Administration (ECA) was a new government agency created to administer the aid funds. The Chief Administrator was equal to the heads of other executive departments and reported directly to the President. To avoid conflicts in what might

---

*H. Bradford Westerfield, in his book *Foreign Policy and Party Politics: Pearl Harbor to Korea* (New Haven: Yale University Press, 1955) points out that this "was a double victory for an administration seeking to cut losses in China." This program not only cut funds, but also involved the Republicans "in a China aid policy," pp. 266-67. It may have caused the administration some concern as well. The possibility that economy-minded appropriations committees might also cut funds for Europe must have occurred to government leaders.

prove to be areas of overlapping jurisdiction, the Administrator was to keep the Secretary of State informed and consult with him on plans having to do with overall foreign policy. If a conflict arose which the Administrator and the Secretary were unable to resolve, the problem was to be referred to the President for final decision.[25]

ECA administrators were to be further helped by the guidance of two advisory groups whose expertise could be relied on during the course of the aid mission's assignment in China. The National Advisory Council on International Monetary and Financial Problems could provide answers to general questions and the Public Advisory Committee for the China Program* could deal with problems specifically pertaining to aid to China.[26]

The man chosen to head both the European Recovery Program and the Economic Cooperation Administration was Paul G. Hoffman. At a time when the American government considered foreign aid one of its most essential commitments, the job was extremely important. Hoffman, said to have been Senator Vandenberg's personal choice for the position,[27] accepted the position with the modest comment, "It seems that I was the least obnoxious of the Republicans."[28] Hoffman had risen from his first work as an automobile salesman in 1911 to be the President of the Studebaker Corporation.[29] He brought to his new post many valuable qualities, "administrative abilities, vast experience in big financial operations, excellent contacts with leading personalities in the country, the highest possible standing in American political life."[30] As his immediate subordinates in the Washington Office, Hoffman chose

---

*Members of the Public Advisory Committee for the China Program were appointed by the Administrator of the program. According to a document published by ECA in February, 1948, called "Economic Aid to China under the China Aid Act of 1948," members of the committee were: "Isaiah Bowman, president emeritus of Johns Hopkins University and a member since 1940 of the Permanent International Commission for China and the United States; Arthur B. Foye, senior partner of the international public accountant firm of Haskins and Sells and, since 1945, president of the Far East-American Council of Commerce and Industry; Paul V. McNutt, former ambassador and United States high commissioner to the Philippines, and president and chairman of the Board of United Service to China; Elizabeth Luce Moore, former chairman of the USO Council, one of the founders in 1940 of United China Relief, and a trustee of Wellesley College, of the China Institute in America, and of the United Board for Christian Colleges in China; and Walter S. Robertson, former minister-counselor for economic affairs at the United States Embassy in Chungking, and a principal assistant to General George C. Marshall during his special mission to China in 1945-1946." *China White Paper*, II, 1015-1016.

W. Averell Harriman as head of the European program and Harlan Cleveland as head of the China program.

Barely thirty when he took over his duties in Washington, Cleveland had already spent eight years in government service. In 1940 he joined the Farm Security Administration hoping to help low income farmers. After World War II he accompanied the Allied Control Commission to Rome to help people in areas ravaged by the war. He spent two years with the commission and another year in Italy with the United Nations Relief and Rehabilitation Administration (UNRRA); an experience which led him to be chosen in 1947 as the director of UNRRA's China program, and to his position with ECA a year later. Intelligent and idealistic, Cleveland was determined to make his life's work count in the struggle for the betterment of mankind. Throughout his time with ECA he tried to place the agency's efforts in the context of overall American policy and to foresee the long-range effects of the program on both China and the United States. His questioning memos on the purposes of the mission not only give great insight into their author but invaluable information on the mission for which he was working and for which he tried to be both annalist and analyst. Given the chaotic conditions in the aid-receiving country and the ambiguous policies of the aid-giving country, making sense out of their relationship proved to be a continuing challenge which Cleveland tried to meet. As head of the Washington office, he worked closely with Paul Hoffman in the United States and with the man chosed to run the aid missions in China.[31]

In April, at a meeting of the Commerce Department's Business Advisory Council, Hoffman asked Roger D. Lapham to take the job of Chief of the China Mission. Lapham, successful businessman, former mayor of San Francisco, and noted for his abilities as an administrator, accepted.

The Economic Cooperation Administration, headed by Cleveland in Washington and Lapham in China, divided the grant for economic aid into three categories: commodity aid, industrial reconstruction aid, and rural reconstruction aid. Roger Lapham, after almost two months of careful preparation, arrived in China in June 1948. He was enthusiastic and confident. The situation he encountered was to prove frustrating, exhausting and discouraging.

Chapter 2 Footnotes

[1] Dean Acheson, *Present at the Creation,* p. 304.

[2] *China White Paper,* II, 372.

[3] Robert A. Dahl, *Congress and Foreign Policy* (New York: W. W. Norton & Company, 1950), p. 60.

[4] *Ibid.*

[5] *China White Paper,* II, full text of the President's statement, pp. 981-83.

[6] *Ibid.* I, 383, See also *Military Situation in the Far East,* I, 397, wherein Marshall again mentions that on his return from China he found it difficult to make long-range plans for China policy.

[7] *China White Paper,* I, full text of Secretary Marshall's statement, pp. 380-84.

[8] Arthur H. Vandenberg, Jr. (ed.), *The Private Papers of Senator Vandenberg* (Boston: Houghton Mifflin Company, 1952), p. 524.

[9] *Ibid.*, p. 523.

[10] U. S., *Congressional Record,* 80th Cong., 2d Sess., 1948, XCIV, Part 3, full text of Senator Vandenberg's speech, pp. 3667-68.

[11] Robert A. Dahl, *Congress and Foreign Policy,* p. 182.

[12] U.S., *Congressional Record,* 80th Cong., 2d Sess., 1948, XCIV, Part 9, full text of General MacArthur's telegram, pp. A1377-78.

[13] Robert A. Dahl, *Congress and Foreign Policy,* p. 61.

[14] U.S., *Congressional Record,* 80th Cong., 2d Sess., 1948, XCIV, Part 3, 3859.

[15] Charles Wertenbaker, "The China Lobby," *The Reporter,* VI (April 15, 1952), 12.

[16] Ross Y. Koen, *The China Lobby in American Politics* (New York: The Macmillan Company, 1960), p. 100.

[17] Paul A. Varg, *Missionaries, Chinese, and Diplomats: The American Protestant Missionary Movement in China, 1890-1952* (Princteon, New Jersey: Princeton University Press, 1958), p. 294.

[18] U.S., *Congressional Record,* 80th Cong., 2d. Sess., 1948, XCIV, Part 9, full text of Congressman Judd's radio broadcast, pp. A56-57.

[19] *China White Paper,* I, 388.

[20] *Ibid.*

[21] U.S., *Congressional Record,* 80th Cong., 2d. Sess., 1948, XCIV, Part 3, full text of Senator Kem's remarks, pp. 3675-83.

[22] *Ibid.*, p. 3692.

[23] *Ibid.*, p. 3671.

[24] *China White Paper,* I, 390.

[25] Harry Bayard Price, *The Marshall Plan and Its Meaning* (Ithaca, New York: Cornell University Press, 1955), p. 69.

[26] *China White Paper,* II, 1015.

[27] William Walton, "Heavy Load for Hoffman," *The New Republic,* April 19, 1948, p. 12.

[28] Jacob A. Rubin, *Your Hundred Billion Dollars: The Complete Story of American Foreign Aid* (Philadelphia: Chilton Books, 1964), p. 44.

[29] *U.S. News & World Report,* April 16, 1948, p. 41.

[30] Jacob A. Rubin, *Your Hundred Billion Dollars,* p. 95.

[31] Biographical Information on Harlan Cleveland from *Current Biography,* 1961 (New York: The H. W. Wilson Company, 1962), pp. 104-106.

Second and third from L.: R. Allen Griffin and Mrs. Griffin; Seventh from L.: Mrs. Lapham; Eleventh from L.: Roger D. Lapham.

Griffin Papers, Hoover Institution on War, Revolution and Peace.

The Situation in China

During the winter and spring of 1948 while American officials debated, passed, and began detailed planning on the aid program, events of great portent were taking place in China. The civil war raged on, but with a significant difference. The Communist armies not only turned the tide in their favor early in the year, but they managed to carry out Mao Tse-tung's military plan in another way. This was the change from guerilla to positional warfare. Chen Po-Ta,* a colleague of Mao Tse-tung's, wrote later:

> Owing to new conditions, new growth of the revolutionary strength, and new changes on the part of the enemy, guerilla warfare was changed into regular warfare as in the last stage of the War of Resistance to Japanese Aggression . . . In the latter period of the War of Liberation, regular warfare developed to such an extent that it included the operations of army corps in which large numbers of heavy arms were employed and attacks of strongholds were launched.[1]

Mao's prediction that this would mark a turning point in history was indeed true.[2]

By the middle of 1948 the Communists controlled nearly all of North China, large areas between the Yellow River and the Yangtze, and smaller strongholds throughout the South. They held most of China's food-growing regions and from these rural areas successfully harassed and interrupted government communications and transportation. Although Chiang's armies still held a numerical advantage in June, the territory they controlled diminished weekly.

Nationalist losses on the battlefield were accompanied by other devastating developments, the most serious of which was the economic crisis. China's inflation had been going on for eleven years and had reached incredible proportions. As one author noted, "In the first eight months of 1948 . . . prices increased more than 6,000 percent."[3]

---

*Chen Po-ta was a member of the Central Committee of the Communist Party of China when he wrote a book in commemoration of the party's thirtieth anniversary in 1951. His book is not without bias, but this passage on the change in the war is accurate.

29

Government expenditures went up at a comparable rate and in May alone reached 75 trillion Chinese dollars. Attempts to solve the crisis met with failure. Monetary reforms proved useless, and when the government resorted to printing money to meet the deficit, prices rose three times as fast as the notes being issued.[4] A simultaneous effort to raise funds through increased taxes not only failed to provide enough money to solve economic problems, it placed the burden on the segment of the population least able to bear it — China's already overburdened peasants.

Faced with huge setbacks in the civil war and with a disastrous economic situation, the Nationalists could not tolerate the loss of popular support. Yet government actions often contributed to the growing discontentment and the subsequent loss of peasant loyalty. Tax increases, for example, which seemed essential to government leaders, drove peasants off the land and robbed them of their livelihood.

Most of China's farmers were sharecroppers who paid for the use of the land by giving the owner a percentage of each crop. When taxes increased, the landowners took a larger share of the peasant's harvest, until, in some cases, the total year's crop went to the landlord leaving the peasant without rice for himself or his family. Unable to make a living, the tenant farmers were forced to leave the land and, as half-starved refugees, jammed into the cities. In the spring of 1948, disastrous droughts and floods throughout the country further exacerbated the plight of the people and they were easy victims for famine and disease.[5] In Canton alone, during a cholera epidemic, over a thousand abandoned bodies were left on the streets in a month's time. One observer noted, "Canton had exactly ten syringes, forty-eight needles, and fifteen medical personnel to give inoculations to a population of two millions."[6] Throughout the country, miseries accumulated for China's people as the government's power to alleviate them diminished.

Undoubtedly, Chiang Kai-shek would have liked to ease the suffering of his people, solve the country's economic problems, and end the civil war. By the middle of 1948, however, he could not effectively control events or institute needed reforms. China's destiny was no longer in his hands, if indeed it had ever been.

During his years as President, he had been challenged by many adversaries who prevented him from establishing complete control over the country. Warlords with their own armies ruled their provinces, the Japanese took Manchuria and later most of China's important coastal territory, while, inland, the Communists consolidated their position and moved to expand their rule.

Faced with this constant harassment, the Nationalist government was able to carry its democratic principles no further than the printed page,* and power rested solely with the Generalissimo and a small, involuted group of men whom he trusted. In an interview with an ECA official, an eminent Chinese historian, Fu Ssu-nien, analyzed Chiang's leadership:

> Gimo's great strength is an indomitable will coupled with stubborn national pride — in this respect he's China's Winston Churchill. His great weakness is insufficient knowledge of modern statecraft — in this respect his mental structure is antediluvian China.

*   *   *

> Now, in the face of fierce communist competition, Gimo's great weakness moved into the fore. His ignorance of modern statecraft left him unable to cope with events. His narrow mindedness protected his relatives in high places. What was needed was up to date administration, good government, enlightened politics — unless he could find these in adequate measure, he might have won the war and lost the peace.[7]

Although Historian Fu clung to the vain hope that Chiang could still, in 1948, establish good government in China, other scholars had shifted their allegiance.

The previous year the Nationalist government, in an effort to control dissension, had banned all anti-government and anti-war propaganda. The resultant repressions were felt primarily on college campuses. Students were beaten and killed when universities were raided, and spying on professors by secret police was common.[8] A teacher at Tsinghua University expressed the disillusionment felt by many. "We have become so completely convinced of the hopelessness of the existing government that we feel the sooner it is removed the better." In as much as the Communists, "are obviously the only force capable of

---

*The Nationalist government was set up in a democratic framework. There were five branches: Executive, Control, Legislative, and Judicial Yuans with a President and Vice-President. Elections were provided for and the Constitution outlined a representative, democratic government.

making this change, we are now willing to support them as the lesser of two evils." The professor also commented on the role the United States was playing in China and pointed out that it seemed to him that there had been a fundamental shift in American policy.

> At one time America apparently wanted a genuinely progressive government in China. During the past two or three years, however, it has seemed to be interested less and less in liberalism and more and more in anything, no matter how reactionary that might be a bulwark between it and communism . . . The result is an American government which talks constantly about democratic rights yet continues to aid a Chinese government increasingly mindless of these rights.[9]

It was made abundantly clear that many Chinese shared the professor's sentiments when anti-American protests increased through the spring of 1948. There were two main issues involved in the protests — American involvement in Japan and the China Aid Act of 1948 which would give more aid to Chiang Kai-shek.

The Chinese feared that America's build-up of Japan would result in a resurgence of Japanese aggression or of the old dreaded notion of an agrarian China, and an industrial Japan. America was accused of taking up where Japan had been forced to leave off on the "New Order" for Asia. Furthermore, according to Dr. Dorothy Borg, the "aim of American policy was generally regarded by the Chinese press as being the reconstruction of Japan to serve as a military and economic base for the United States in a war against the Soviet Union."[10]

The China Aid Act, which was intended to give a modicum of relief to China's misery, proved to be a source of further dissension. According to one observer, it "reinforced the tie between the United States and the increasingly unpopular and apparently moribund government of Chiang Kai-shek," and caused "the most widespread and outspoken anti-American movement up to that time."[11]

In May and June, 1948, student riots broke out throughout the country and continued for many weeks. John M. Cabot, American Consul General in Shanghai, commented on the riots and implied the students did not appreciate America's largesse on their behalf. He warned that as a result of the protests many taxpayers might wish to stop all aid to China, including aid to the universities and to students who had been the beneficiaries of American help for many years.[12]

Ambassador J. Leighton Stuart also was alarmed at the violence and the intensity of the criticism. One of the few ambassadors who knew the country to which he was assigned better than the country he represented, Stuart had been born in China in 1876 and had spent fifty-three of his seventy years in his adopted country. Beginning as a teaching missionary at Nanking Theological Seminary, he soon was appointed President of Yenching University, the post he retained until 1946 when he became the American Ambassador.[13]

His alarm over student protests was founded on his familiarity with the country's traditions and his long years as an educator. As he wrote later, Chinese students are "an excellent barometer of popular trends" since they are "the most highly sensitized element" of the population. "Their reactions are more intelligent and spontaneous, and they have fewer inhibitions. Chinese students are as a class passionately patriotic."[14]

Convinced, then, that the riots and demonstrations were no mere outbreak of youthful exuberance, Stuart tried to reach the protesters with a statement explaining America's intentions and denying that the United States planned to help rebuild Japanese imperialism. The United States, most emphatically, would not re-establish the military power of Japan and only wanted to "restore enough of Japanese economic life to enable the Japanese people to become self-supporting." If they were not economically self-sufficient they would be a "liability not only to the United States but also to China" and would, as a consequence, be in a situation "made to order for Communism."

The Ambassador exhorted the students to carefully examine their consciences and to face their deepest motives. "If you are not true to yourselves then most assuredly you cannot be true to any one or any thing else."[15]

In spite of Stuart's experience, sincerity and good intentions, the statement was pedantic and scolding. According to Dr. Dorothy Borg, "Many Chinese felt it an affront to personal and national dignity that diplomatic representatives of the United States felt free to threaten and rebuke the citizens of China." And the results were not those the Ambassador hoped for. "The students, including those of Dr. Stuart's own university, Yenching, responded with strikes, demonstrations, and written declarations of their resentment, and were supported by many faculty members." To "further protest" students and teachers also started "a campaign . . . to refuse all American relief supplies." [16]

* * *

Into the midst of this rampant anti-American movement in a country ravaged by war and economic chaos, Roger Lapham and the ECA mission arrived in Shanghai early in June 1948. There were many reasons for the mission on which they were embarked, reasons which somehow made more sense in Washington than in China. The aid was designed to give the Nationalist government a "respite," and "stay of execution," so it would have time to institute needed reforms. At the same time, the United States hoped to keep the goodwill of the Chinese people, obtain some strategic raw materials, counterbalance Russia's interests in Asia, and placate administration critics at home.

Chapter 3 Footnotes

[1] Chen Po-ta, *Mao Tse-tung on the Chinese Revolution* (Peking: Foreign Languages Press, 1953), p. 42.
[2] Mao Tse-tung, *Selected Works 1945-49* (5 vols.; New York: International Publishers, 1954), V, 157.
[3] Harry Bayard Price, *The Marshall Plan and Its Meaning*, pp. 182-83.
[4] *Ibid.*
[5] Jack Belden, *China Shakes the World* (New York: Harper & Brothers, 1949), p. 100.
[6] Roger Pelissier, *The Awakening of China, 1793-1949* (London: Secker and Warburg, 1963), p. 473.
[7] Conversation between James Ivy, ECA official, and Chinese historian Fu Ssu-nien. Copy in a paper entitled "Postmortem," n.d., in R. Allen Griffin Papers, Hoover Institution on War, Revolution and Peace, Stanford, California. (Box numbers, which ordinarily would be cited, have not yet been assigned to the Griffin Papers by the Hoover Library). This collection will hereinafter be cited as the Griffin Papers.
[8] Roger Pelissier, *The Awakening of China*, p. 491.
[9] Derk Bodde, *Peking Diary: A Year of Revolution*, (New York: Henry Schuman, Inc., 1950), p. 24.
[10] Dorothy Borg, "America Loses Chinese Good Will," *Far Eastern Survey*, XVIII (February 23, 1949), 43.
[11] Tang Tsou, *America's Failure in China, 1941-50*. (2 vols.; Chicago: The University of Chicago Press, 1963), II, 478.
[12] Excerpt from Cabot's statement in Dorothy Borg, "America Loses Chinese Good Will," *Far Eastern Survey*, p. 43.
[13] John Leighton Stuart, *Fifty Years in China: The Memoirs of John Leighton Stuart, Missionary and Ambassador* (New York: Random House, 1954), p. 347.
[14] *Ibid.* p. 188.
[15] Copy of Stuart's statement to the Chinese students, *China White Paper*, II, 869-70.
[16] Dorothy Borg, "America Loses Chinese Good Will," *Far Eastern Survey*, pp. 43-44.

ECA — Plans and Personnel

The head of ECA's China mission, Roger D. Lapham, had been in the country twice before. In 1937 he had spent three weeks in Shanghai and Peking, and in 1947 he had stopped briefly on an around-the-world tour, but, as he admitted, he was not an old China hand nor an expert on the country.[1] He was, however, a very successful American businessman, affable and expansive, who hoped to use his extensive administrative skills to run an efficient program for both the United States and China.

Lapham was born in 1883 in New York City. His father was a partner in the Texas Company, but the interests of his mother's family were to be a greater influence in his life. She had five brothers who were sea captains and it was in their business, the American-Hawaiian Steamship Company, where he spent his life. He graduated from Harvard in 1905 and moved to California where he worked in various jobs for the family company. After service with the Infantry in World War I and almost a year in London with the United States Food Administration, under Herbert Hoover, Lapham returned home. During his absence a company of which W. Averell Harriman was Chairman of the Board, had made extensive purchases in his family's shipping business. These inroads by Harriman's company, accompanied by foreign competition, placed the American-Hawaiian Steamship lines in jeopardy. In 1925, however, Roger Lapham became president of the company, moved its headquarters to San Francisco, and restored it to its former eminence in the shipping industry. From 1938 to 1943, he served as Chairman of the Board. During World War II, he was a member of the National War Labor Board and in 1944 was elected Mayor of San Francisco. Although a lifelong Republican, he ran for mayor as an independent, promised he would serve only one term, eschewed allegiance to any political power base. After an eventful four years, which included the organization of the United Nations in his city, Lapham retired from office in January, 1948. Six months later he was in Shanghai.[2] A large, white-haired man whose exuberance belied his sixty-five years, Lapham tackled his job as head of ECA's China mission with confidence and optimism. "His genial manner and friendly chattiness," however, as Ambassador Stuart correctly surmised, "sheathed a shrewd competence which those who dealt with him learned to respect."[3]

In the two months before his departure for China, Lapham and other aid planners carefully outlined the kind of program they envisioned. They soon found that the experience of the United Nations Relief and Rehabilitation Administration provided a recent example of what ECA hoped to avoid.

* * *

After World War II, UNRRA began sending aid to countries suffering from the war. Fearful that the aid efforts would be misconstrued as an attempt to impinge on the sovereignty of the receiving countries, UNRRA shipped aid goods to port cities and turned it over to the various governments for distribution. Problems that were rarely encountered in other places arose immediately in China. Distribution costs were unusually high because of the huge land areas and the poor transportation. Aid goods which were to be given to the Chinese people were sold on the black market for exorbitant amounts. The equitable distribution envisioned by UNRRA leaders was further frustrated by the lack of price controls or rationing systems. Harlan Cleveland, who was appointed head of UNRRA's China program in 1947, recalled that they had:

> Tried to spend two-thirds of a billion dollars in a country that lacked transportation and trained people, and was in the midst of a civil war and a raging inflation. It was just too much; when I arrived in Shanghai . . . I found evidences of indigestion all over the docks of that crowded port . . . When scholars later theorized about the limits of "absorptive capacity" for aid, I thought I had perhaps been witness to the clearest case in which the outsiders had tried to do too much too fast with too little cooperation from the insiders.[4]

In China it was true, as one ECA economist later remarked, "You can't put much in and you can't take much out."[5]

Other difficulties arose for UNRRA when its efforts, like those of the Marshall Mission, became the basis for Communist invective. Although both missions avowed the most equitable and impartial intentions toward the Nationalists and the Communists, in each case, Chiang Kai-shek's government received preferential treatment.

UNRRA's aim was to help people in war-ravaged areas without consideration of their race, creed, or politics. As George Woodbridge, who has written the history of UNRRA states, in China the effort to make a fair distribution became a "most formidable issue." Faced with Chiang's natural reluctance to help his enemies, and forced to deal with his regime as their distributing agency in the country, UNRRA could do little. The course they followed "was to exert continuous pressure upon the Government to distribute equitable quotas of UNRRA supplies to the people in Communist-controlled areas." This effort "was, however, successful only to a slight degree."[6]

By the middle of 1947, approximately two percent of supplies sent to China went to the Communist areas.[7] Of the percentage they received, the Communists complained that the goods were often inappropriate and useless. "Following one of these shipments UNRRA became famous throughout the Liberated Areas as the organization which tried to rehabilitate the peasants of Shantung with mouldy chocolate and spoiled cigarettes."[8]

Displeasure with their disproportionate share of supplies went hand in hand with their growing contention that UNRRA had become an organization devoted to furthering imperialism. According to a Communist report, "Although there was plenty of direct interference in the Chinese civil war by the American Army and . . . State Department . . . it left American policy wide open to the charge of meddling into other countries' internal affairs." Not wishing to be accused of such interference, the United States found UNRRA to be useful in "camouflaging American assistance to Chiang's civil war." UNRRA had thereby "been degraded from the status of an international institution to that of an instrument of the American State Department and of an organ of the Truman doctrine in China." The report concluded:

> Friendship for the American people continues because the Chinese people believe friendship between them exists, but they draw a line between the American people and the present American policy. They demonstrate against it because they are bitter. Chiang Kai-shek and Truman are sitting in the same tank for which UNRRA has provided part of the fuel, and the people recognize their common enemies.[9]

If they were aware of this report, it is unlikely that ECA officials expected they would eventually be the object of similar attacks. They were much more concerned when their mission began with avoiding the more obvious pitfalls of UNRRA. Each part of the new program was designed to anticipate and avert problems the international organization had encountered. Special emphasis was to be placed on supervision of aid materials from beginning to end. There was to be no leaving of supplies on the docks where they might waste or fall into the wrong hands.

The Commodities program would be limited to a few important, basic items. These would be distributed to a specific number of cities close to the coast; they would be directly useful to the people and the use to which they were put would be carefully observed and duly reported. The commodities the planners decided on were food, petroleum products, cotton, and fertilizer. The cities where these were to be distributed were Shanghai, Tientsin, Peking,* Canton, Swatow, and Nanking. The food was to be distributed to dispersal points and handed out under a rationing program. The cotton and petroleum were to meet the needs of specific cotton mills, and of selected industries and transportation facilities. They were to be carefully dispensed and their end-use closely supervised. Fertilizers were harder to control as far as distribution and end-use were concerned, but planners hoped that careful checks would solve this problem.

The second part of the program, Industrial Reconstruction and Replacement, was to be kept small, precise and controllable. The total reconstruction of China's industries would have cost many billions of dollars more than the China Aid Act provided. The planners decided, therefore, to concentrate on coal supplies, electric power facilities, and railroads in an effort to improve the most serious problems faced by China's industries. Before implementation of this important part of the mission, detailed surveys of the areas of greatest need were to be made. In the course of these surveys, mission officials decided that this part of the program needed more expertise than was to be found in China, and agreed that an American engineering firm must be employed to set up the projects and train Chinese to run them.

The third part of the program, Rural Reconstruction, was to be supervised as meticulously as the others. A Joint Commission of

---

* Peking (Northern Capital) was called Peiping (Northern Peace) during the aid mission's activities in China. In the interests of consistency, however, the city will be called Peking in this book, except in direct quotes.

Americans and Chinese would concentrate on a few projects where the most good could be realized in the least time.[10]

On July 3, 1948, the aid agreement was signed by Ambassador J. Leighton Stuart and the Chinese Minister of Foreign Affairs, Wang Shih-chieh.[11] For months American officials had been requesting and suggesting that the Nationalist government make drastic reforms. They demurred, however, from writing specific reform measures into the aid agreement. The State Department explained in 1949:

> It would have involved the American Government, in effect, in an attempt to force the Chinese Government to do in its own self-interest those things which only that Government itself was in a position to initiate and which, in the last analysis, only the Chinese Government itself could administratively perform.[12]

The agreement, therefore, differed only slightly from those signed at the same time with countries in Europe. The primary differences centered around price controls, rationing, and attempts to overcome the problems of inflation. The Chinese government, for example, agreed to what was called the "principle of jointness" under which each major decision about the aid program had to be the product of joint agreement between the two countries. This caused delays in the administration of the program, but seemed the only way the United States could avoid assuming total responsibility for the dispersal of aid, yet retain control of some part of it. To try to deal with the inflation problems, the Chinese government agreed to a "counterpart" fund for handling their share of expenses. Since the value of large deposits of Chinese money in the fund would have diminished rapidly, it was agreed that the Chinese government would make its deposits only on the request on ECA. Writing in January, 1949, Harlan Cleveland stated, "If this had not been done, the deposits made against the first $20 million worth of ECA goods shipped would by now have depreciated to the equivalent of less than half a million dollars."[13] The governments also decided that part of the funds to be expended would keep a constant value compared to a stable measure such as American dollars or cotton yarn. These funds were specifically for administrative costs or the longer range projects, such as rural and industrial reconstruction. This seemingly reasonable part of the agreement unexpectedly added to inflation at times, and ECA officials soon learned that deciding when and where the money should be spent took careful consideration. Dr. Dorothy Borg, who had recently returned from China, wrote:

> To pump money or commodities in the form of wages into any given area tends to disrupt the local economy unless it is offset by the purchase of a substantial quantity of supplies. Few areas in China, however, produce sufficient surplus to permit large-scale buying.[14]

At times American officials found themselves in the position of exacerbating the very problems they were in China to try to mitigate. These experiences were ahead of them, however, on the day the agreement was signed and ECA's programs began in earnest.

* * *

To assist him in administering the mission, Roger Lapham asked an old friend, R. Allen Griffin, of Monterey, California, to be his deputy. Griffin, born in Kansas City, Missouri, in 1893, was a graduate of Stanford University where he had been editor of *The Quad* and founder and editor of the *Stanford Illustrated Review*. In 1919, after serving two years in the Infrantry, he became a reporter for the Portland *Oregonian*, then the Portland *Journal*, and later in the year became secretary to Prince Lubomirski, Poland's first minister to the United States. During the next two years, Griffin acted as director of the Polish Bureau of Information and as manager of the American Polish Chamber of Commerce. In 1921 he began what was to become his life work when he established the *Peninsula Herald* in Monterey.

Six months before Pearl Harbor, Griffin re-enlisted in the Army and during the war served as public relations officer on the staff of Lieutenant General Ben Lear, as assistant chief of staff G-2 in the Second Army, and as commanding officer of the Thirteenth Infantry Regiment of the Eighth Infantry Division. He returned to his publishing and radio businesses after the war until Lapham asked him to serve as Deputy Director of the China Aid Mission.[15] Ambassador Stuart called him a "fine combination of American practicatity and idealism."[16]

At the end of the mission, Griffin wrote a series of articles for his newspaper which outlined China's history, described the situation in the country, and related his experiences as an ECA official. Although he had not been in China before the mission, he was a discerning observer and like many others before him, he left with a great respect for the Chinese people.

> They have endured through the thousands of years, cultivated through their own abilities a civilization of such fine quality that its influences have deeply affected the art and artisanship of the civilized world for centuries. They have maintained their individual racial traits through thousands of years as no race in history. They have the capacity to rebound from untold suffering. They are refreshed by a wonderful sense of humor. They are the largest resource of quick-to-learn labor in the world. Poor as they are, sick as they are, illiterate as they are — they are a truly great and admirable people.[17]

Although they were not "do-gooders,"[18] both Griffin and Lapham hoped the aid program which they were about to undertake in June, 1948, could be of help to the admirable Chinese people. They hoped, moreover, to improve on America's previous experiences with aid to China by running an efficient and businesslike operation. Since both men were wealthy and successful and motivated by neither the need for money nor employment, the challenge of the mission was both inducement and reward. They would be assigned to an exciting part of the world where they could use their considerable talents in the service of their country. And, as Allen Griffin wrote in a letter to his daughter, it was an opportunity to "be in the midst of some history that is in the making and to be taking part in it."[19] In the course of their year in China, they were to travel over 30,000 miles carrying out their mission and trying to meet its challenges.

The duties they performed were both divergent and overlapping. Roger Lapham was responsible for liaison with other American representatives in China, dealings with agencies of the Chinese government, and contacts with the ECA office in Washington. Allen Griffin, making use of his many years in the newspaper business, was in charge of public relations. The two men also shared responsibility for the day-to-day operation of the program and supervision of people in the various field offices.

Mission headquarters for Roger Lapham, his staff and advisors were set up in Shanghai with regional offices in Peking, Tientsin, Tsingtao, Canton, Nanking, and Taipei, Taiwan. These regional offices telegraphed weekly, semi-weekly, and monthly reports to the Shanghai office reporting aid activities in each city. A cumulative monthly report, subsequently sent from Shanghai to Washington, relayed information on arrivals, releases, and balances on hand for the commodity program and progress reports for the industrial and rural programs. Besides factual information, the reports included a rundown of the problems encountered, impressions of Chinese associates, the effectiveness of ECA operations, requests to the Washington office, and suggestions on American policy. Since many of the men associated with ECA had been in China with earlier missions, their accounts were particularly helpful to Lapham and to aid leaders in Washington as well.

Chapter 4 Footnotes

[1] Roger Lapham, "The Chinese Situation as I Saw It," Address to the Commonwealth Club of California, San Francisco, September 8, 1949. Copy in R. Allen Griffin Papers.

[2] Biographical information on Roger Lapham from *Current Biography, 1948* (New York: The H. W. Wilson Company, 1949) pp. 364-66.

[3] J. Leighton Stuart, *Fifty Years in China*, p. 190.

[4] Harlan Cleveland, *The Obligations of Power: American Diplomacy in the Search for Peace* (New York and London: Harper & Row, Publishers, 1966), p. 105.

[5] The ECA official quoted in Dorothy Borg, "ECA and US Policy in China," *Far Eastern Survey*, XVIII, 199.

[6] George Woodbridge, *UNRRA, The History of the United Nations Relief and Rehabilitation Administration* (3 vols.; New York: Columbia University Press, 1950), p. 382.

[7] *Ibid.*, pp. 388-89. See also Chinese Liberated Areas Relief Association Information Department, *UNRRA Relief for the Chinese People* (Shanghai: July, 1947), p. 11.

[8] *Ibid.*, p. 12.

[9] *Ibid.*, p. 30.

[10] Description of the proposed aid program, *China White Paper*, II, 1010-1012.

[11] Copy of the aid agreement, *China White Paper*, II, 994-1001.

[12] *Ibid.*, I, 394.

[13] Harlan Cleveland, "Economic Aid to China," *Far Eastern Survey*, XVIII (January 12, 1949), p. 5.

[14] Dorothy Borg, "ECA and US Policy in China," *Far Eastern Survey*, XVIII, p. 199.

[15] Biographical information on R. Allen Griffin from *Current Biography*, 1951 (New York: The H.W. Wilson Company, 1952), pp. 245-46.

[16] J. Leighton Stuart, *Fifty Years in China*, p. 191.

[17] R. Allen Griffin, "China Changes Dynasties," *Monterey Peninsula Herald*, August 17, 1949. The series ran from July 20, 1949, to August 17, 1949. Copy in Griffin Papers.

[18] Interview with R. Allen Griffin, January 20, 1971.

[19] Letter from R. Allen Griffin to Mrs. E. C. Goossen, August 12, 1948. Griffin Papers.

ECA'S Commodity Program

In addition to setting up administrative offices, one of ECA's first duties was to take over the operations of its predecessor. The China Relief Mission had been allocated $45,000,000 to operate from June, 1947, to June, 1948. Although in actual operation since October, it had initiated many relief projects, and, of special importance, had started a rationing program for rice and wheat in the major cities. ECA took over the rationing program, employed many members of CRM, including director Donald L. Gilpatric, and absorbed its remaining supplies. According to Harlan Cleveland, CRM provided "a ready-made nucleus for ECA's operations in China." [1]

THE COMMODITY PROGRAM

The Commodity Program was meant to help the Nationalist government maintain order in strategic cities by providing food, petroleum products, and employment (in textile mills). Fertilizer distribution to rural areas was included in the hope that new crops would also increase essential food supplies.

As soon as the aid agreement with China was signed in July, 1948, the mission began to implement part of the Commodity program. ECA took over operation of the rationing projects which had been in existence under CRM since April and the distribution of food continued uninterrupted.

ECA ORGANIZATION CHART

Washington Office
Paul Hoffman, *Head*
Harlan Cleveland, *China Mission*

China Office
Roger D. Lapham, *Head*
R. Allen Griffin, *Deputy*

Regional Directors
Henry T. Samson — Canton
Philip K. Crowe — Nanking
Ritchie Davis — Peking
James T. Ivy — Tientsin
Peter Hopkins — Tsingtao
Loris Craig — Taipei

Program Directors

| *Food* A.M. Hurt | *Petroleum* C. Osborn | Commodities *Cotton* Harry Witt | *Fertilizer* A. Viola Smith | IRR* Charles Stillman | JCRR** Chiang Mon-li T.H. Shen Y.C. James Yee Raymond Moyer John E. Baker |

*Industrial Reconstruction and Rehabilitation
**Joint Commission on Rural Reconstruction

Food — ECA's $70,000,000 allotment for rice, wheat and flour was to be used for distribution among 12,000,000 people in six cities. The agreement between the Chinese and American governments stated that 40 per cent of the food would be provided by ECA and 60 per cent by the Chinese from indigenous sources. ECA's counterpart, the Council for United States Aid (CUSA)* formed an Office of Emergency Food Procurement (OEFP) to obtain supplies for its share of the program. The government's Ministry of Food (MOF) would lend its assistance as well. The projected plan agreed on by ECA and the Nationalist agencies stated that first quarter (July-September, 1948) supplies would be furnished by both ECA and CUSA (OEFP, MOF). Second quarter (October-December, 1948) provisions, after the fall harvest, were to be furnished primarily by the Chinese. During the remaining two quarters in 1949, the responsibility for food acquisition would again be shared, with ECA providing for any deficits the Nationalists could not meet. As will be seen, this plan, like many others optimistically initiated, was impossible to implement.

Food distribution and sales were made through established commercial warehouses and retail shops.[2] The rations were given out month to month, or as one ECA report stated, "hand to mouth," [3] and were based on census figures in each city. If, for example, a man in Peking wished to obtain food through ECA's program, he went to a district official's office for a ration coupon, then to a designated shop to make his purchase. Flour, which was distributed in Peking and the other northern Chinese cities, was shipped through Tientsin from Shanghai. Rice for the southern cities was also dispersed from the Shanghai docks.

Initially, leaders of the American mission hoped that the profits from food sales could be used by the Chinese to purchase more food.

*The Council for United States Aid (CUSA) was set up by the Nationalist government and was staffed by a distinguished list of Chinese. Premier Wong Wen-hao, Chairman; O. K. Yui (Yu Hung-chun), Governor of the Central Bank, Vice-Chairman; Wang Shih-chieh, Minister of Foreign Affairs; Wang Yun-wu, Minister of Finance; Yu Ta-wei, Minister of Communications; Chang Kai-ngau, former Central Bank Governor; Tsu-yee Pei (Pei Tsu-yi), head of the technical mission to Washington; K. C. Wu (Wu Kuo-chen), Mayor of Shanghai; Yen Chia-kan, former Commissioner of Finance in Taiwan Province; Cheng Tao-ju, former CNRRA Deputy Director-General; Pi Hsien-pi, Director of the Secretariat; Chou Yum-feng, Deputy Director of the Secretariat; Chen Kwan-yuan, Director of the Material Procurement Department; and Li Ku-chin, Director of the Department of Planning and Auditing. *Chinese News Service,* June 8, 1948.

These hopes were soon extinguished, however, as procurement of food and payment became incredibly difficult for both the Chinese government and ECA. These efforts, like all others, were inextricably interwoven with China's economic problems. ECA's Progress Report in August described the worsening situation:

> The general index of wholesale commodity prices registered an increase of 500% in the short space of a little less than three months . . . The (black market) exchange rate of the U.S. dollar which stood at CN$1,150,000 at the beginning of June, rose to CN$12,000,000 on the eve of the currency reform on August 19th. For the first time., the facilities of Government operated printing presses were found inadequate to cope with the urgent demand for banknotes, and by mid-July, notes of as large as CN$1,000,000 to CN$5,000,000 denominations had to be released for circulation.[4]

The economic chaos was further complicated by the fact that these exchange rates were not only changing rapidly, but were different in various sections of the country. In the south of China, near Canton, the free market rate of Chinese dollars to American was 6,000,000 to 1, near Shanghai 13,000,000 to 1, near Peking 15,000,000 to 1.[5]

In August the Nationalist government enacted reform measures to try to meet the crisis. All foreign exchange, Chinese national currency, gold and silver bullion were called in and exchanged for new currency called the Gold Yuan (GY) which was to be fixed at a rate of four to one American dollars.

As an added reform measure, the government froze commodity prices. The initial agreement between ECA and China called for realistic pricing, so the market price of rationed food would be no more than 5 per cent below the open market price. When the Nationalists set the August 19 ceiling on grains and set the rationed food rate 50 per cent below the ceiling, the idea of realistic pricing favored by ECA, was annulled. This move violated the aid agreement which had called for consultation between ECA and the government before changes were made. Annoyed by the unilateral action, ECA officials withdrew from the rationing program temporarily. They felt the government's policies undermined their efforts to help stabilize China's major cities.[6] As ECA's report stated:

> By fixing such without ECA concurrence, at rates less than 40-50 per cent of the prevailing market prices in July and August, sales resulted in turning the program into a pure subsidy for millions of people who could well afford to pay higher prices.[7]

The government's price fixing, which ECA officials deplored, had other unfortunate consequences. Rice growers refused to sell at the lowered rates, and when they did sell their produce, they compensated for the low prices, by a "15 to 20 per cent grit and dirt adulteration." [8]

Less than a month after the currency reforms were introduced, commodity prices began to rise and confidence in the new Gold Yuan soon diminished. Money was quickly put in the market to obtain scarce goods, this in turn put pressure on the price structure, and the dizzying spiral began again.

ECA ended its temporary withdrawal from the rationing program on September 1 and resumed food distribution in Shanghai, Peking, Tientsin, Swatow, Canton, and Nanking. Meanwhile, Tsingtao had been added to the list of aid receiving cities and the same month an emergency food relief program was set up briefly in Mukden.

Communist troops held this Manchurian city under siege, so supplies for Nationalist troops and the city's population were brought in by air. Six hundred to one thousand tons of ECA flour [9] were delivered and were "cooked and fed directly to key groups of workers, particularly in the arsenal and coal mine." [10] Although these food supplies undoubtedly alleviated the suffering of the people to some extent, one eyewitness reported that rationed food lasted "a worker only ten days out of every month." As a result, many people had to eat "the large Manchurian soybean cakes, ordinarily used only for cattle and fertilizer."[11]

John Melby, who worked for the American Embassy in Nanking, traveled to Mukden in September and recorded his impressions in his diary:

> Mukden is grim, desolate and hungry. The marks of starvation on the people are becoming dreadful. No one walks fast or smiles, all have that yellow hunger look. It is terrible to see a great city die and it cannot conceivably be much longer before it falls. That will be the end of Manchuria.[12]

Conditions in the city grew worse daily until the two Nationalist armies stationed there were ordered to evacuate.* Challenged immediately by the Communists, they surrendered. In a few short weeks

---

*The two armies stationed in Mukden were among the best-trained troops the Nationalists had. They were the New First and the New Sixth; the New First had been led and trained by American General Joseph W. Stilwell during World War II.

Chiang Kai-shek lost almost half a million men[13] and, as American Consul in Peking, O. Edmund Clubb, wrote later, "mountains of American military supplies" were taken over by the Communists as well.[14]

The ECA distribution officer, Donald L. Moore, left the city on October 29 and the airlift of emergency food supplies from the American aid mission ended the same day.[15]

Meanwhile, the food programs for the other cities had run into a variety of difficulties. Shipments of flour destined for the Tientsin-Peking area to fulfill the needs for the last half of October amounted to only 12,000 of the required 30,000 tons.[16] The balance of the October amount was not delivered until near the end of November. Part of the problem was the difficulty of getting ships to carry supplies from Shanghai to the northern cities. The Chinese Ministry of Communications made agreements with several private shippers to transport the flour, but before the agreement could be carried out, military officials of the government took over the ships for their own use. Fearing this might happen to them, other shippers hid their vessels and refused to allow them to be used by the Ministry of Communications.[17] One branch of the government, ECA soon learned, could cancel agreements made by another and frustrate the carefully laid plans for efficient food distribution.

As a result, Peking's rationing program was soon behind schedule. The September allotment was not dispersed until October 25. The flour which eventually arrived at the port of Tientsin had to be transported overland from there to Peking with further delays en route. When supplies finally arrived, rationing officials had additional problems obtaining horse carts to take the flour from the godowns (warehouses) to the shops. In spite of previous agreements the number of carts which appeared for work decreased daily, making an adequate distribution almost impossible. ECA's monthly report from Peking complained also of the problem of "tips" * required by warehouse coolies and cart owners who demanded them of the shop owners and delayed releases of the commodities if their wishes were not granted.[18]

*This was an application of the ancient facet of Oriental life called "squeeze," which was deplored by most Americans and understood by them as a manifestation of rampant corruption and graft. Thomas E. Dewey traveled through the Far East in 1951. This is his description of what he found out about the practice: "I gained my first real understand-

These problems in Peking, as elsewhere, were accompanied by the need to feed huge and growing numbers of people. Thousands of student refugees in the city increased the food ration needs every day. The students admitted that they over-registered for ration coupons because the food obtained this way was the only food they had. In Peking 6,000,000 coupons were issued in September for 2,000,000 people.[19] Officials, who ordinarily would have taken action against over-registration, hesitated to do so with the students. Their actions were probably stayed by the ancient Chinese reverence for scholars and by their awareness of the power of student unrest.

ECA's rationing program in the city of Tsingtao suffered from many of the same difficulties encountered in Peking. Huge numbers of refugees were entering the city from the surrounding countryside, which was controlled by the Communists, and the vital shipments of food were late and inadequate. When supplies finally arrived, the equitable distribution envisioned by ECA was thwarted by some of the city's officials. It was not unusual in China for government officials to use commodities to gain political favor with certain groups they wished to influence.[20] The monthly report from Tsingtao noted:

> During the latter half of September and the first week of October, the Tsingtao press was unfavorable to and highly critical of the Ration Board and this no doubt caused the authorities to seek a formula to mollify the "Popular" clamor. It is significant that adverse press criticism ceased entirely after the announcement that journalists would be granted extra rations.[21]

This misuse of ECA supplies by city officials was reminiscent of UNRRA's experience and represented a situation aid planners had hoped to avoid with the new relief mission.

Meanwhile, in Shanghai and Nanking the rationing programs were also behind schedule. In October only one-fourth of the needed rice

---

ing of 'squeeze' in Hong Kong. In America we call it graft but in China it is part of everybody's pay, from houseboys to government officials. Nobody is paid a living wage; everybody is expected to make something on the side. An American who had lived in Hong Kong for many years put it this way: 'I tell my houseboy to go out and buy me a hat. The houseboy, though he is completely honest and trustworthy, will make five per cent on the hat. It's the rule. The trouble begins only if my boy takes twenty per cent, thirty or forty per cent. That's bad. He's broken the rules; he is corrupt and must be dismissed. Five per cent is proper, more is stealing." Thomas E. Dewey, *Journey to the Far Pacific* (New York: Doubleday & Company, Inc., 1952), p. 196.

MAP I
ECA HEADQUARTERS AND REGIONAL OFFICES

Peking
Tientsin
Tsingtao
CHINA
Nanking
Shanghai
(Headquarters)
Taipei
TAIWAN
Canton

MAP II
CITIES IN ECA'S COMMODITY PROGRAM

Mukden
Peking
Tientsin
Tsingtao
CHINA
Nanking
Shanghai
TAIWAN
Canton
Swatow

Scale of Miles

0   1000

supplies were available. John Melby noted in his diary that in the Nationalist capital city of Nanking:

> In six weeks food prices have gone up five hundred per cent and today they are changing hourly. Since the August economic decrees rice has been disappearing and now there is almost none to be seen or bought in the towns. People stand in endless lines day after day, usually fighting, squabbling, tangling with the police, and now and then wrecking a rice shop.[22]

When the situation Melby described was not alleviated by November, food riots broke out in both Nanking and Shanghai. The urban unrest ECA had hoped to prevent through commodity distribution had erupted in alarming proportions. Roger Lapham and Allen Griffin moved quickly to try to avert what could grow into a national crisis. They obtained an emergency loan of 10,000 tons of rice from Governor General Alexander Grantham of Hong Kong, acquired supplies from Bangkok,* and stepped in to barter for stocks which in some cases had been withheld by provincial governments.[23] In addition, they arranged for eleven ships with rice cargos to go to Tsingtao, Peking, and Tientsin.

The November crisis was averted momentarily although five of the seven cities in which the rationing programs were functioning continued to suffer from problems of one kind or another. Only the Canton and Swatow programs were successful from their inception, primarily because food procurement was handled by the provincial government. The governor of the province where these two cities were located was T. V. Soong who cooperated enthusiastically with ECA.**

---

*Siam had a bumper rice crop in 1948 and ECA negotiated for the purchase of large amounts. Letter to Colonel Elliot W. Thorp, American Embassy, Bangkok, Siam, dated February 18, 1949 from R. Allen Griffin. (Griffin Papers).

**T. V. Soong, Chiang Kai-shek's brother-in-law, had held important financial, diplomatic, and political posts for the Nationalists since 1928. He had been Finance Minister, Foreign Minister, and Premier at various times in his career. From 1947 to 1949, he was the Governor of Kwangtung Province where he was a large landowner. In spite of his long and active career for the government, the Generalissimo did not completely trust him. Soong was aware of this and described one incident in their relationship to R. Allen Griffin. In order to run his province more efficiently, he had acquired several small airplanes. They would enable him to oversee provincial activities in remote areas and to collect supplies and taxes. When Chiang heard of this, he confiscated all of the planes and told Soong not to buy others. "You are not," he was commanded, "to establish a private air force." Interview with R. Allen Griffin, January 20, 1971.

When the central government did not provide its share of the food, the government of the province supplied the deficit and the rationing program functioned smoothly.

Elsewhere the issue of food procurement became the source of considerable annoyance to ECA officials when the Chinese agencies proved unable to acquire their agreed share. According to ECA's October report, the Ministry of Food and the Office of Emergency Food Procurement were "totally inadequate and inefficient."

The report went on to admit that the agencies were beset with many problems: transportation from farming areas was erratic and insufficient, local authorities were not always willing to allow food commodities to leave their areas, farmers often refused to sell at government prices or to accept GY currency, military requisitions of food took precedence, and economic chaos delayed every phase of procurement and payment.[24]

This was an accurate list of the problems faced by the Chinese agencies and seemed, above all, to indicate that their food procurement failures were due to circumstances over which they had no control. They had no authority, for example, to force farmers to sell their produce; nor could they improve transportation or solve China's economic problems. ECA officials, however, continued to blame the Office of Emergency Food Procurement and the Ministry of Food. The October report stated that the OEFP in "its three months existence proved completely and disastrously inadequate to its appointed tasks of civilian food procurement. Its failure to meet Government commitments is seriously jeopardizing the program at a time when food sufficiency is of the utmost importance." [25]

ECA complaints persisted into November when the monthly report charged that, "The very confusion that OEFP was supposed to prevent has been aggravated by the added confusion within OEFP itself." [26] Chinese procurements were very low at the time, especially for the Peking-Tientsin area where, of the needed 1,300,000 bags of flour, OEFP was able to obtain only 100,000 bags. The author of the report again acknowledged that the Chinese agencies had many problems but concluded that they could not be absolved from their poor performance.

> Hardships notwithstanding, OEFP has never since its formation performed the functions of civilian food procurement agency in a manner

which could be considered satisfactory after due allowance for all problems involved. The continuance of that organization under its present direction and mismanagement constitutes a menace to the successful execution of the . . . ration program.[27]

Although similar ECA complaints appeared in later monthly reports, procurement problems eased somewhat in December, and the January report was able to proudly announce that the programs in "Shanghai, Nanking, Canton, Swatow and Tsingtao enjoyed complete freedom from supply problems." [28] In February and March as well the programs were completed within the calendar month.[29] The two northernmost cities, Peking and Tientsin, had been captured by the Communists and were removed from the rationing program. This eased food procurement for the remaining cities, which was further relieved by increased supplies after the fall harvest, removal of price ceilings, and frequent price changes to adapt to the inflation. Ration prices were changed every ten days at this point in the program.

Although the difficulties related to the acquisition of food were alleviated somewhat by these circumstances, other difficulties arose and ECA officials were never able to enjoy a trouble-free program. The barter methods for the procurement of rice, for example, which had seemed to be a successful means to deal with farmers who had been reluctant to sell their rice for GY currency, proved to be the source of a major imbroglio. In most cases, ECA representatives bartered directly with the farmers. In November, however, an agreement between ECA, CUSA, and the Farmer's Bank of China was signed. The Farmer's Bank was to obtain rice from farmers in exchange for certificates. The certificates were to be exchanged the following spring for fertilizers which would arrive in China by January, 1949, for distribution in February. By the time the fertilizers were to be distributed, ECA officials found out that the bank had collected little rice from the farmers, had purchased rice on the open market causing further shortages in the city, and had paid for the rice with funds borrowed from OEFP, which, according to its members, had been short of operating money from the beginning. In spite of this, the bank told ECA it had outstanding certificates covering several thousand tons.

The ECA monthly report stated:

Our own investigations proved that not only had they never even printed the certificates, but they had never even approached the farmers who were supposed to have their certificates. The Bank planned, without consulting ECA-CUSA and in complete disregard of their agreement, to ship our fertilizer to Taiwan for profitable use or sale.[30]

The agreement was hastily cancelled, but the incident increased the American officials' distrust of Chinese institutions and further undermined their confidence in contractual arrangements.

After the bank crisis was averted, other problems required the attention of ECA officials. In Nanking, essential rice polishing equipment could not run because of a shortage of electrical power. ECA intervened and persuaded the power company to provide rice millers with enough current to get through the emergency. At the same time, in Canton and Swatow the previously efficient rationing program broke down when a new governor took office. The former governor, T. V. Soong, had cooperated enthusiastically with ECA ration officials, but the new governor, General Hsueh Yueh, had not proved willing to provide the same procurement facilities. ECA had to acquire additional provisions for both cities. Meanwhile, OEFP, which had been unable to meet its procurement responsibilities earlier, had all its funds stopped while a new cabinet was being formed by the central government.

ECA's problems were ultimately resolved by the Communists when they took over in one city after another during the first five months of 1949. A report from Tientsin described the end of ECA's operations:

> Distribution of flour to the ration shops was carried on right up to Friday, January 14th; though during the period between December 14th and January 14th distribution to certain areas . . . had to be discontinued because these areas were under direct shell fire; the carters refused to enter these areas, and we were unwilling to send our inspectors into them because of the dangers involved. On January 14th *all* deliveries were stopped. We were then left with about 130,000 bags of flour still in mill warehouses: 93,000 in CTC godowns, and 4770 tons of wheat still unmilled in the various mills. Later, all of these stocks were confiscated, and all plans for a ration distribution were perforce abandoned.[31]

James Ivy and Durand Wilder, ECA's senior officials in Tientsin, tried to prevent aid supplies from being seized when, on the 28th of January, they were informed that the Communists were 'borrowing' 80,000 bags of ECA ration flour. The following day, having confirmed that this was true, they called on the Mayor to complain. The Mayor's office refused to admit the Americans and referred them to the

Foreign Affairs Bureau which had been set up by the Communists. In his report, James Ivy wrote:

> We told Mr. Ch'en of the Foreign Affairs Bureau that since this ECA flour was taken without our knowledge or consent, we could only regard it as a "theft" of U.S.E.C.A. property (Mr. Wilder didn't know the Chinese word for "confiscated"); and that we would have to report it as such. We pointed out that we had been told the Liberation Party would respect property rights; that, while if we had been consulted, we might have agreed to a special ration for workers in essential industries, we would also have explained the basic principle of a *general* ration which ECA has maintained to date. We pointed out, too, that on occasions we had prevented, by vigorous protests, the confiscation for military use of this same flour by the Nationalist Garrison Commander; insisting that ECA commodities were for the benefit of the common people, *not* the military.[32]

This conference with the Foreign Affairs Bureau did not, however, bring about the return of American supplies. Shortly thereafter, ECA's Legal Office prepared a paper on the "illegal seizure and question of title to the commodities seized" at Peking and Tientsin, but this protestation proved no more effective than the complaints of Ivy and Wilder.[33]

In the ensuing months as the cities in which ECA operated were lost by the Nationalists, the pattern was repeated and stocks were appropriated in much the same manner. In April, Nanking fell; in May, Shanghai and Tsingtao. The southern cities of Swatow and Canton were not taken over until the following autumn and in those two cities the rationing programs had ended before the Communists arrived. Shanghai was the only city on the mainland where ECA continued to operate on a limited basis after the Communists were in power. In the spring of 1950, ECA supplies in Shanghai were ultimately confiscated.

Petroleum Products — After agreement was reached with the Chinese government, this part of the aid program was set up through companies already operating. Four companies were primarily involved, The Standard Vacuum Oil Company, Shell Company of China, Ltd., California Texas Oil Company, and the Chinese Petroleum Corporation.[34] Petroleum products were to be used for transportation, industry, power plants, and homes. Little crude oil was produced in China, so importation was vital and became increasingly so as coal supplies were cut off by the Communists.

ECA's administrative problems were fewer on this commodity than the others because shipping, the means of internal distribution, and end-use reports were provided by the oil companies which had been operating in China for many years. Problems with this part of the commodity program stemmed, therefore, not from excessive squeeze, distribution for political purposes, procurement, or other difficulties which plagued the food program, but rather from payment to the oil companies.

The overall program had been divided into three parts. The first two parts, amounting to about $22,000,000, were financed out of bonded stocks owned in China by the oil companies. This was handled through the Central Bank of China. The Chinese government had prohibited remittance in dollars for expenses connected with internal distribution. The companies, aware of inflation in the GY currency in which they were required to be reimbursed, raised their billing prices to the bank. This price increase exceeded the rate allowed by the American Government.

> As a result, the Central Bank found itself unable to provide dollar exchange to release additional stocks for consumption in China and, at the same time, unable to secure reimbursements from ECA for stocks previously financed in dollars.[35]

The Chinese government ultimately allowed one of the companies dollar remittance instead of GY and as a result the oil company agreed to rebill for the previous deliveries.*

This seemed to resolve the major difficulties for the moment, but problems with foreign exchange rates continued to be of concern and in December, ECA advanced $15,000,000 to the Central Bank so it could continue to finance the program. Just before the end of the year, however, this procedure was abandoned and arrangements were made for financing petroleum releases and future shipments through

---

*These accounts were not settled several months later. In a letter to Harlan Cleveland, Allen Griffin urged ECA to settle the account. "We have been so upset by the failure of ECA to approve the repayment or 'advance' or what-have-you of the 12 million dollars due the Central Bank of POL [Petroleum, Oil, Lubricants] purchases, that we sometimes wonder whether our conceptions of business ethics are crooked or whether Washington's is a little off the mark . . . I can only add that failure to repay this money, on the slim excuse that the oil companies have not completed their documentation, is a source of the greatest personal embarrassment to Roger and myself." (Letter to Harlan Cleveland, Washington, dated May 11, 1949, from R. Allen Griffin, Canton. Griffin Papers.)

American banks. At the same time, ECA required its approval in advance for each release or shipment. This was to assure that no supplies were stockpiled and carried out a policy started in September when ECA tried to have no more than a thirty-day reserve in any one place.[36]

This policy was not without its drawbacks as an ECA report noted:

> Oil is not something that can be handed out from day to day as needed, and accordingly it is quite likely that some ECA-financed petroleum products will fall into the hands of persons not friendly to the Nationalist Government. We hope that we shall not be criticized if this occurs as we are making an earnest effort to maintain stocks in Nationalist areas . . . not in excess of 30 days' supply.[37]

By January, 1949, the major portion of unconsumed stocks were in Shanghai and Taiwan and were distributed from there throughout the remainder of the program. Relatively little of this commodity, which had been paid for out of ECA funds, fell into Communist hands.

Cotton — China's textile industries were the largest in the country,* and ECA hoped to help supply raw cotton to the mills to keep them going for several reasons. First, the major mills in Nationalist areas were in Shanghai, Tsingtao, and Tientsin. Keeping the mills operating and people employed, especially in Shanghai, would contribute to quelling urban unrest. Second, the yarn and cloth made from the cotton could be used for domestic purposes and for exportation. Third, the money gained from the sales of the cotton products could be used to buy more raw cotton and eventually, if the plan succeeded, the textile industry would be economically sound within the country and its products a valuable foreign exchange asset.

Before the war, China had had little need to import raw cotton since most of it was grown within the country. By 1948, however, domestic cotton reached urban mills only sporadically, primarily because of the disruption of transportation. Raw cotton provided by the aid program became the major source at this time. The first bales reached the mills in October and by the end of the year almost 300,000 bales had been imported, and $52,000,000 of the $70,000,000 allocated by Congress had been spent.[38]

*In 1946 they were second only to the United States in production: United States, 1,873,000 metric tons—China, 896,000 metric tons. John Kieran (ed.),*Information Please Almanac, 1949* (New York: Doubleday & Company, Inc., and Garden City Publishing Co., Inc., 1950), p. 87.

The report of an official group sent from Washington to observe ECA activities stated that the cotton program was one of the best and likely to continue to be worthwhile because of its direct help to the city economies. In a rather qualified statement, the report added, "The procedure is the best that can be provided unless ECA should undertake physically to execute the entire program."[39]

Even the barter efforts with this commodity proved successful.* An agreement with the Netherlands East Indies provided for $10,000,000 in cotton cloth to be exchanged for $5,000,000 in cash and $5,000,000 in rubber. Half the rubber in turn would be used in China and the balance would be sold to the United States to be stockpiled. Under this contract, the first shipment of textiles left Shanghai in November and by January, sales had brought $4,500,000 to China.

Cotton products were used for barter within the country as well. More than 2,000 bales of yarn and cloth were traded in Nanking, Shanghai, and Nanchang for rice at a time when little grain was moving from the producing areas.[40]

In January the fear that cotton products would get into the hands of the Communists caused officials in Washington to call a halt to shipments, and for several weeks the only bales received at China's ports were through direct purchase from India.[41] ECA administrators, upset over the disruption of the cotton program which they felt was one of the most effective, tried to persuade the Washington office to allow shipments to be resumed. Roger Lapham, who was in the United States for two months in the early part of 1949, succeeded in convincing officials of the need, and in March, American aid cotton again arrived in China.[42] Allen Griffin wrote Lapham that "the release of the cotton program had a most desirable effect." [43]

The same month, however, the most devastating inflation on this commodity since the mission had started made it almost impossible for this to continue to be a program helpful to China's economy. One type of yarn used for spinning went from GY94,000 on March 1 to GY555,000 on March 31, another type went from GY530,000 to GY3,070,000.[44]

---

*(It will be remembered that barter agreements had not always materialized for ECA. See p. 78.)

At the end of April word was again received from Washington that all shipments were to be stopped. Paul Hoffman cabled ECA headquarters in China:*

> I understand about 51,000 bales of cotton scheduled to arrive Shanghai on 17 ships during next 35 days . . . I feel strongly that diversions cotton ships now scheduled to arrive . . . should be ordered immediately and that ECA financed goods on ships that already have arrived should not be unloaded in Shanghai.[45]

American aid to China's cotton industries in Tsingtao, Tientsin, and Shanghai came to a halt immediately. ECA supplies were confiscated almost at once, except in Shanghai where, at the end of June:

> ECA cotton stocks totalled 24,000 bales of raw cotton valued at about $4 million, 49,000 pieces of cotton cloth valued at approximately $300,000, and 45,000 bales of cotton yarn due from the mills in exchange for raw cotton furnished them by ECA, valued at about $10 million.[46]

These stocks were frozen for many months and ultimately seized by the Communists in the spring of 1950 when all residual supplies were taken over.[47]

Fertilizers — The fertilizers were intended originally to increase China's rice crop, but since they were not to be used until the fateful spring of 1949, events prevented them from being helpful to the Nationalists.

Unaware that their efforts were futile, however, ECA's committee worked throughout the fall months on negotiations for procurement and distribution. Originally the committee hoped to obtain all needed fertilizer in China, but since domestic production amounted to only 81,000 tons of the needed 500,000 tons, importation became imperative.[48] Hurried negotiations were started to obtain fertilizers from America. Fertilizer acquisition by American farmers rose sharply after the first of each year, so negotiators hoped to acquire the supply for China before the end of December to avoid causing shortages in the United States.

These negotiations and others were the major activity of the Fertilizer Committee. In October, for example, Miss A. Viola Smith and Mr. Edward Shim, who were the Acting Head of the program and its

---

*Cables, like telegrams, use an abbreviated form of language. The many cable quotations in this paper adhere to this shortened form, unless clarification seemed necessary.

technical adviser, respectively, spent most of their time "in active participation in 15 meetings of ECA-CUSA Cereal and Fertilizer meetings; Working Party meetings and Central Trust meetings . . . each of many hours duration." [49] In November as well, their report listed the meetings and again added they were "each of many hours duration." [50] The procedure continued in December and by January fertilizers had finally been contracted for, but none had arrived. Again the fear that they would be taken over by the Communists, or as the monthly report stated, "fall into the hands of unauthorized persons," held up the program.

The first shipment arrived in February and was designated for use to redeem the certificates issued by the Farmer's Bank.* More shipments arrived in March, but were difficult to transport to the planting areas. After the Communists crossed the Yangtze in April, this part of the commodity program, which had barely begun, ended for the mainland. All further distribution of fertilizer under ECA took place on Taiwan.

Supplies Left Over from the China Relief Mission — Although food, cotton, petroleum products, and fertilizers were the commodities designated for distribution under the China Aid Act, ECA also inherited stocks of pesticides and medical supplies from its predecessor. Pesticide allocations were discussed at meetings between American and Chinese representatives in September, 1948, and led to the following agreement on dispersal:

> 35 percent of these pesticides to the Joint Rural Reconstruction Commission, 15 percent to the Ministry of Agriculture and Forestry for free distribution at agricultural demonstration centers, and the remaining 50 percent for sale through commercial channels.[51]

CRM's medical supplies, worth approximately $5,000,000, arrived periodically and by the end of 1948 almost 90 per cent were in China. Fears that these supplies might be taken over by the Communists, however, prevented their dispersal throughout the country, and they were used primarily in Shanghai, Canton, and Taipei.[52]

Coal — China's coal reserves, estimated to be the fourth largest in the world,[53] were more than adequate for the needs of the country. By

*This was when the Farmer's Bank incident was discovered.

the fall of 1948, however, the huge supplies of the Manchurian mines were controlled by the Communists and the Kailan mines north of Tientsin, which provided almost half the supply for the Nationalist areas, were also threatened. In these mines and others remaining in Nationalist hands, production was very low. According to the report of an American senator who was assessing the situation on China, the mines were producing five and a half million tons a year[54] when Shanghai alone needed one and a half million.[55] Under the circumstances, reserves in many eastern cities dwindled to dangerously low levels, and, though coal was not part of its commodity program, for a brief period ECA was involved in emergency procurement.

Admiral Oscar C. Badger commanded the United States Naval Forces in Tsingtao. In November, 1948, finding the city's coal reserves would last only approximately two weeks, the Admiral appealed to General MacArthur in Tokyo to send emergency supplies to relieve the city's plight.* In an exchange of cables, the General refused and Badger turned to ECA for help. After many involved negotiations between ECA, Washington, and Tokyo, MacArthur finally agreed to allow a minimal shipment to go to China. The report of one ECA official stated that the General was persuaded to allow coal purchases only on the basis that it was for the "normal course of business and *not an emergency involving military operations and supplies.* **" [56] The tentative agreement arranged for 15,000 tons to be shipped to China each month.[57] This provided a minimum requirement for Tsingtao while the city's Fuel Commission and ECA continued to try to obtain additional supplies from other sources in China.[58]

---

*Tsingtao was not, it will be remembered, one of the six original aid-receiving cities on ECA's list, but in September, 1948, the port was included as a recipient of commodity aid. As Allen Griffin noted in a letter to a friend, "The port of Tsingtao gets especial ECA treatment because of the presence of the fleet there. We added about 100,000 refugees . . . in a special program of free feeding, due to the fact that refugees are pouring in vast numbers into the city because of Communist activities and by feeding them we keep them quiet. Besides, it wouldn't look very good if Chinese starved within sight of the U.S. flag in that harbor at a time when the U.S. was spending $275,000,000 in China. Then, because of the jeopardy to the city if the power plant and industries ran out of coal, we have been procuring coal in order to keep Tsingtao from becoming discontented. As a matter of fact it has been a fairly expensive business to maintain a suitable environment for the U.S. Navy." Letter to Captain Frank T. Watkins, Commandant, Naval General Line School, Monterey, California, from Allen Griffin, dated December 17, 1948. Griffin Papers.

**Underlining in memorandum written by Charles L. Stillman.

Aid was sent to Tsingtao until the advance of the Communists no longer made it possible. In April the Navy went afloat and American operations in the city ended soon after.

END OF THE COMMODITY PROGRAM

The same month, when the Communists crossed the Yangtze with ease, Admiral Badger advised ECA officials to move to a safer distance from the advancing armies. Mission leaders decided, therefore, to settle in Canton and, by April 29, Roger Lapham and Allen Griffin had begun to establish a new headquarters office.

The small residual contingency they left behind in Shanghai was headed by George St. Louis. In late April and early May, St. Louis conferred with the American Consul General and an international group called the Shanghai Assistance Committee. They agreed to try to keep the city running smoothly until the Communists took over. Primarily, they intended to supply food to people who were connected with essential industries, utilities, and public services, such as police and firemen. John Keswick, of the British company Jardine-Matheson, expressed the goals of those who stayed in Shanghai in a letter to Allen Griffin. Keswick had been appointed as head of the Shanghai Assistance Committee and wrote he was accepting the job "in the hope that I may be able to help the people of Shanghai to receive the food which is being given to them by E C A , and to try to find ways and means of keeping the utilities and industries in operation for the benefit of the citizens of this great town."[59]

Before leaving for Canton, Griffin wrote Harlan Cleveland describing conditions in the former headquarters' city, and explaining why he felt ECA's regional office should remain open:

> In Shanghai the expenses of handling incoming cargoes and the yarn that we are endeavoring to find safe-haven for, plus the expenses of the bankrupt organizations that have to do with rationing and food distribution, require approximately US$20,000 a day, according to St. Louis and past CUSA records. All costs have become higher week by week as our income in local currency has become less. Washington must accept a situation that requires the vesting of complete authority in the Regional Director to handle US funds according to his own best judgement to meet his particular operational problems. This is mandatory, and I urge you most strongly not to hold back in this respect. St. Louis is being advised not only by the Consul General, but by an international committee of competent men. In an important sense our remaining operations

in Shanghai are simply to support an imponderable position — that of up-holding the remaining good people, American, Chinese and Western Europeans, in maintaining that city in a state short of chaos so long as it is not Communist-occupied. I think it is worth the money and the effort, and it is one place where we can uphold our dignity and our prestige until the end if we will only remain bold enough to play the game on behalf of the best remaining influences there. It would be a sorry day if we sold them short, and in my opinion it would have a disastrous result on our already suffering American prestige.[60]

Officials in Washington agreed with Griffin's recommendations and St. Louis was allowed to handle dispersement of supplies belonging to ECA.

On May 25, Shanghai fell. In the weeks that followed the Communists seemed to be taking over somewhat more slowly than in other cities. Perhaps they wished to show some deference to the many foreign business interests centered there, or perhaps their previous experiences had made them more cautious. When they moved into Tientsin in January, ECA official James Ivy, had noted that, "The military occupation was well planned, well organized and well executed. But the civil administration seems not nearly so well prepared. A great lack of competent administrators, executives and officials is evident." Some of those who took over large Nationalist organizations seemed "to lack education and training, and certainly are lacking in experience." This was true not only in their dealings with Chinese institutions, but with foreign interests as well.

No one at a high official level is ready to meet or talk to any foreign consular officials or businessmen. There is no evidence of any plan for the future resumption of import and export business, on any basis. The Customs is not operating, though most of the Customs personnel are still on the job. The whole city, as far as foreigners, relations and foreign trade are concerned, is a vacuum — a vacuum in which all foreigners simply sit waiting, wondering what the future may bring.[61]

The evident lack of experience and experienced personnel, which Ivy described, may have caused the Communists to decide to attempt a more gradual approach in their takeover of foreign interests in Shanghai. At any rate, an ECA report late in June noted that:

Although no disposition has yet been made of the raw cotton, yarn and cloth, indications are that the Communist attitude toward ECA in Shanghai may be more conciliatory than in Peiking and Tientsin where there was outright confiscation of ECA food and textile stocks. Significant straws in the wind have been the resumption by the textile mills of yarn deliveries to ECA and the release by the Communist authorities of 350,000 empty rice and flour bags which ECA sold immediately to cover operating expenses. Plans for disposal of the cotton, yarn, and cloth are now being discussed by the Shanghai Regional Office with the Shanghai Assistance Committee and the Joint Management Board (taken over by the Communists).[62]

The conferences continued for many months without any decision being made on the final dispersal of ECA's commodities. In November, 1949, Roger Lapham, who had been back home in San Francisco since July, received a letter from June Dagny Nergaard describing life behind the "Bamboo Curtain." Miss Nergaard had been George St. Louis' secretary for four months after the Communists took over and had left to visit her sister in the United States. She wrote that there were no longer food shortages in the city since routes to the countryside had been opened, and that, although inflation persisted, "it does not spiral as wildly as it did under the Nationalist regime." When she resigned, "there were 3 Americans left in ECA: Mr. St. Louis, Mr. Stubbs (Administration) and Mr. Koenig (Accounts) and 20 of the alien staff." The Shanghai Regional Office was "in the process of liquidation and closure, of course." Negotiations had continued and finally, "Plans have been evolved for the disposal of the $20,000,000 worth of cotton; and with the Joint Management Board acting as unofficial mediator between ECA and the Communists, attempts at unfreezing it are underway." [63]

The plans, however, did not work out. George St. Louis left Shanghai in the spring of 1950 when all negotiations ceased and the Communists confiscated the residual assets ECA had hoped to keep out of their hands.* On his return to Washington, St. Louis wrote Griffin that

---

*Apparently the Communists did not consider this the end of all aid from America. Less than a fortnight after the confiscation of ECA stocks, Communist officials approached George St. Louis and told him that "upwards of 40,000,000 people were adversely affected by famine conditions and that the situation was more severe than at any time since the turn of the century." Although St. Louis noted, as had Miss Nergaard, that there were no food shortages in Shanghai, other sections of the country were suffering. The officials approached St. Louis to find out if "religious and philanthropic groups in the United States might be willing to provide relief supplies for the stricken people in the famine areas. Moreover," the ECA official "was repeatedly urged by the Chinese to discuss the famine situation and China's relief needs with the appropriate U.S. Government officials on his . . . return to Washington." After several meetings with the officials, St. Louis told them that he was certain he could not persuade ECA

actually "Shanghai wasn't too tough," and that he had been "angered, frustrated, jubilant, embittered, optimistic and 'down in the dumps' — but seldom bored."[64] His departure marked the end of ECA's existence in the original headquarters' city. Elsewhere on the mainland, the commodity program had long since ceased to operate.

***

As a part of ECA's efforts, the commodity aid had not made significant changes in China's economy, nor had it altered the course of the civil war. Its main accomplishment had been the distribution of provisions which for a brief moment alleviated the suffering of some of China's huge and needy population. The food distributed by ECA had kept people from starving.[65] The cotton program had kept the mills running and had provided employment for a short while. The pesticides, medical supplies, petroleum products, and coal contributed to improving conditions in some areas. Commodity aid, however, had not proved to be a significant means of easing China's problems.

Chapter 5 Footnotes

[1] Harlan Cleveland, "Economic Aid to China," *Far Eastern Survey,* XVIII, 2.

[2] United States, *Economic Cooperation Administration Mission to China, Progress Report, No. 1* (June-July-August, 1948). Griffin Papers. Hereinafter cited as *ECA Progress Report.* Subsequent reports were called monthly reports and will be cited as *ECA Monthly Report.*

[3] *ECA Monthly Report, No. 2,* (October, 1948), Griffin Papers.

[4] *ECA Progress Report, No. 1* (June-July-August, 1948), Griffin Papers.

[5] U.S., Congress, Senate, Report of the Joint Committee on Foreign Economic Cooperation, *China,* December 3, 1948, 80th Cong., 2d Sess., 1948, p. 8. This was a report of a Congressional Watchdog Committee which had representatives in China in the fall of

---

headquarters or the State Department to provide relief supplies unless he had more specific information. He suggested, therefore, that he prepare a questionnaire on which they could present "certain basic statistical data and the answers to certain obvious policy questions." The Communists agreed, so St. Louis prepared the list of questions and submitted it to "Han Ming who expressed his appreciation, promised to secure the requisite information, and gave assurances that he would transmit it to the writer at ECA Headquarters, Washington, D.C.; pointing out, however, that it would probably take some time to sound out higher Communist authorities." Nothing was to come of these negotiations since the same month St. Louis was reporting on them, the war in Korea began and the schism between the United States and China widened. The little known fact, however, that the Communists made even this slight overture for American aid is interesting. Economic Cooperation Administration, Mission to China, Shanghai Regional Office, *Observations on Communist China,* by George St. Louis, June 7, 1950. This information was submitted by St. Louis to the State Department. Copy in Griffin Papers.

1948 to observe and report on ECA activities for the purpose of deciding whether or not aid should continue to be sent to China. Hereinafter cited as Report of the Joint Committee, *China.*

⁶ Dorothy Borg, "ECA and US Policy in China," *Far Eastern Survey,* pp. 199-200.

⁷ *ECA Progress Report, No. 1* (June-July-August, 1948), Griffin Papers.

⁸ *ECA Monthly Report, No. 2* (October, 1948), Griffin Papers.

⁹ *China White Paper,* II, 1022 says one thousand tons; Report of the Joint Committee, *China,* p. 10 says six hundred tons.

¹⁰ *Ibid.*

¹¹ Derk Bodde, *Peking Diary,* pp. 50-51.

¹² John F. Melby, *The Mandate of Heaven: Record of a Civil War, China 1945-49* (Toronto, Canada: University of Toronto Press, 1968), p. 283.

¹³ C. P. Fitzgerald, *The Birth of Communist China,* p. 108.

¹⁴ O. Edmund Clubb, *Twentieth Century China* (New York and London: Columbia University Press, 1964), p. 290.

¹⁵ *ECA Monthly Report, No. 2* (October, 1948), Griffin Papers.

¹⁶ *Ibid.*

¹⁷ Report of the Joint Committee, *China,* p. 9.

¹⁸ *ECA Monthly Report, No. 2* (October, 1948), Griffin Papers.

¹⁹ *Ibid.* See also John F. Melby, *The Mandate of Heaven,* p. 282.

²⁰ Dorothy Borg, "ECA and US Policy in China," *Far Eastern Survey,* p. 199.

²¹ *ECA Monthly Report, No. 2* (October, 1948), Griffin Papers.

²² John F. Melby, *The Mandate of Heaven,* p. 285.

²³ *ECA Monthly Report, No. 3* (November, 1948), Griffin Papers.

²⁴ *ECA Monthly Report, No. 2* (October, 1948), Griffin Papers.

²⁵ *Ibid.*

²⁶ *ECA Monthly Report, No. 3* (November, 1948), Griffin Papers.

²⁷ *Ibid.*

²⁸ *ECA Monthly Report, No. 5* (January, 1949) Griffin Papers.

²⁹ *ECA Monthly Report, No. 6 and No. 7* (February and March, 1949), Griffin Papers.

³⁰ *ECA Monthly Report, No. 6* (February, 1949), Griffin Papers.

³¹ United States Economic Cooperation Administration, Tientsin Regional Office, *General Situation Report of Tientsin for February 1 – March 19, 1949.* Copy in Griffin Papers.

³² *Ibid.*

³³ *ECA Monthly Report, No. 7* (March, 1949), Griffin Papers.

³⁴ *China White Paper,* II, 1025-26.

³⁵ Report of the Joint Committee, *China,* p. 12.

³⁶ *China White Paper,* II, 1026.

³⁷ *ECA Monthly Report, No. 5* (January, 1949), Griffin Papers.

³⁸ *China White Paper,* II, p. 1024.

³⁹ Report of the Joint Committee, *China,* p. 11.

⁴⁰ *ECA Monthly Report, No. 5* (January, 1949), Griffin Papers.

⁴¹ *ECA Monthly Report, No. 6* (February, 1949), Griffin Papers.

⁴² *ECA Monthly Report, No. 7* (March, 1949), Griffin Papers.

⁴³ Letter to Roger Lapham dated February 25, 1949, from R. Allen Griffin. Griffin Papers.

⁴⁴ *ECA Monthly Report, No. 7* (March, 1949), Griffin Papers.

⁴⁵ Cable to Roger Lapham from Paul Hoffman, dated April 25, 1949. Griffin Papers.

⁴⁶ *Status of ECA Operations in Shanghai,* June 23, 1949. Griffin Papers.

[47] Economic Cooperation Administration, Mission to China, Shanghai Regional Office, *Observations on Communist China* written by George St. Louis, June 7, 1950. Griffin Papers.

[48] *Memorandum on Continuation of United States Aid to China, 1949.* Griffin Papers.

[49] *ECA Monthly Report, No. 2* (October, 1948), Griffin Papers.

[50] *ECA Monthly Report, No. 3* (November, 1948), Griffin Papers.

[51] *China White Paper,* II, 1028-29.

[52] *Ibid.,* p. 1028.

[53] John K. Fairbank, *The United States and China,* p. 213.

[54] *Report of D. Worth Clark, Consultant to Appropriations Committee of the U.S. Senate, on Financial, Economic and Military Conditions in China, and Recommendations Concerning Future Aid.* n.d. (Hornbeck wrote "1948" on the report and Clark mentions being sent to China by the committee in September. The report is discussed in the *New York Times,* November 21, 1948, so it is likely it was submitted to the committee the same month). Copy in Hornbeck Papers.

[55] *Memoradum on Continuation of United States Aid to China, 1949.* Griffin Papers.

[56] Memorandum to Roger D. Lapham and R. Allen Griffin from Charles L. Stillman, November 22, 1948. Griffin Papers. Underlining in memo.

[57] *China White Paper,* II, 1028.

[58] Memorandum to Roger D. Lapham and R. Allen Griffin from Charles L. Stillman, November 22, 1948. Griffin Papers.

[59] Letter from John Keswick to R. Allen Griffin dated April 28, 1949. Griffin Papers.

[60] Letter from R. Allen Griffin to Harland Cleveland dated May 11, 1949. Griffin Papers.

[61] United States Economic Cooperation Administration, Tientsin Regional Office, *General Situation Report of Tientsin for January 10-31, 1949.* Griffin Papers.

[62] *Status of ECA Operations in Shanghai,* June 23, 1949. Griffin Papers.

[63] Letter from June Dagny Nergaard to Roger Lapham, November 15, 1949. Griffin Papers.

[64] Letter from George St. Louis to R. Allen Griffin, June 7, 1950. Griffin Papers.

[65] Derk Bodde, *Peking Diary,* p. 171.

ECA'S Reconstruction Projects

INDUSTRIAL RECONSTRUCTION AND REPLACEMENT

The Reconstruction Survey Group, appointed to recommend aid projects for this part of the program, arrived in China with Roger Lapham on June 7, 1948. The group consisted of Charles L. Stillman as chairman, who was a Vice President and Treasurer of *Time*, Inc., four engineers, two economists, and one lawyer. They were to spend the next few months traveling about the country selecting projects to receive American aid.

Use and distribution of the commodity part of the aid program had been fairly easy to determine, according to Harlan Cleveland, however, "In the case of industrial reconstruction, it was impossible to tell from 10,000 miles away what types of industrial development would make the most sense in China's changing circumstances." [1] The committee's decisions were further complicated by the fact that China was not an industrialized nation. As pointed out by Dr. Dorothy Borg, "The level of electrification alone was no more than one-tenth of Mexico's." [2] The few industries which had been developed in the country before the war had been damaged successively by the Japanese, by bombing raids of the Chinese and American forces, and by both sides in the civil war. Besides this devastation, major industries had been weakened by the decreased involvement of foreign nations due to the war and the end of extraterritoriality. The absence of the foreigners was felt most acutely in China's industrial development since this is the area where they had been most actively involved, both in operation and in development. Their absence was also reflected in the higher costs and diminished services in river shipping, since, after the war, foreign ships were not allowed on China's rivers. [3]

The Survey Group traveled extensively in the country in June and July. Two important recommendations grew out of their findings. First, they decided that most of the aid money should be spent on replacement, rather than reconstruction. Second, they recommended that an American engineering firm be employed to supervise the program. The first recommendation recognized the overwhelming needs of China's industry and concluded that for the sake of expediency and efficient use of aid money, repairs should take precedence over the building of new industries. On September 1, at a news conference, Yen Chia-kan, Chief CUSA liaison officer, announced the first projects selected by the Survey Mission. Four major industries would be allocated $4,400,000. Of this amount, the Yangtze Power Company was to receive $1,200,000. Dr. Yen explained that this company serviced "the inadequate Nanking and Tseshyuen plants," and would be a "major factor in stimulating industrial activity, maintaining steady employment and adding to the output of manufactured products." The second recipient, the Kailan Mines, would receive $1,000,000. According to Dr. Yen, the mines were important because they were the "chief fuel supply source for both North and Central China." Aid money would be used to replace equipment "which had deteriorated to a point which threatens the collapse of mining operations." The third project, the Tientsin-Peking Power Grid, was to receive $1,200,000 which would enable it to serve the vital industries of the area. The fourth grant of $1,000,000 was to go to the Taiwan Sugar Company. Dr. Yen explained that this industry had "loomed as a high project of the Stillman survey group because of its value in the export field." [4] At the same news conference, Charles Stillman expressed his conviction that, "It is upon the improvement of China's industrial capacity that the Chinese people will benefit in every walk of life." [5]

The survey group's second recommendation, that an American engineering firm be employed to supervise the projects, reflected a desire to fill the gap left by trained foreign personnel and a recognition of China's need for people with experience and expertise in industrial development and management. The survey group recommended, therefore, that each project employ a private engineering firm to help with the planning, to train Chinese to do the work, and to supervise the initial development. The group further recommended that an American management engineering firm should be employed to coordinate, supervise and oversee the entire industrial reconstruction program.

It was an innovative recommendation which had not been tried in other aid-receiving countries and, according to Harlan Cleveland, "The procedure represents a fresh and encouraging start on a new pattern for publicly financed industrial projects in underdeveloped areas. The problem of grafting branches of Western technology on the great trunk of Asia's agrarian economy is one of the stupendous tasks of this century." [6]

The management engineering company chosen to oversee China's industrial rehabilitation was the J. G. White Engineering Corporation of New York. The Company signed a contract with the Chinese government in October, 1948, and a week later sent a technical group to China headed by Henry Tarring, Jr. ECA's monthly report for October described how the arrangement would work, using the Yangtze Power Company project as an example:

> The Yangtze Power Company has been provisionally allotted $1,200,000 by ECA for replacement work. It has employed Andersen Meyer & Co. as its project engineer. Andersen Meyer will work out project details, specify materials and equipment to be procured, and in what country they are available, the cost of such materials and justification for their use, time schedule for the work, etc. Andersen Meyer's engineering procurement requirements will be submitted to the Technical Group [J. G. White] for review. The Technical Group will either return it to Andersen Meyer for revision, or recommend its acceptance . . . As work develops on the power project, the Technical Group will, from time to time, inspect the job to ascertain that it is proceeding under terms of the contract. The same procedure will be used for each replacement project in ECA's program. Each beneficiary will employ a project engineer; each project engineer will submit its plans to the Technical Group, which is responsible to the ECA-CUSA joint committee. Such a system of graduated controls and responsibilities by engineering experts assures that work will be done efficiently at minimum cost. Such an end should benefit both the Chinese and American peoples. The Chinese people want to see their economy bolstered as much as is possible. The American people want to see their dollars spent efficiently in the interests of the Chinese people. [7]

In October, fourteen more projects were announced, [8] and planning for others went forward until December 21, 1948, when Paul Hoffman announced that this section of the aid program was to be stopped. Communist victories and the diminished area in which the Nationalists were in power made planning for industrial development almost impossible. "At the time of suspension, all the projects were still in the preliminary engineering stage, no funds having been actually committed for procurement." [9]

The only part of the aid appropriation spent on IRR was for the extensive surveys of China's industries made by Stillman's group and for investigation of the possibility of acquiring strategic materials needed by the United States. The Chinese government had agreed to allow the mission to obtain contracts for resources available in China, primarily tungsten, antimony, and tin. Limitations on funds caused American officials to forego the acquisition of tungsten and antimony for stockpiling, but they hoped to get tin and tin concentrates. The survey group conducted the initial investigations and decided to procure the metal from provinces in South and Southwest China, particularly Yunnan.[10]

> Such procurement . . . — to the extent it could be developed — would, in addition to increasing the supplies of minerals needed by the United States, serve the double purpose in China of increasing local employment and augmenting the country's slender foreign exchange resources.[11]

There were problems with inflation, a shortage of mining equipment, and inadequate transportation involved in the acquisition of tin, but preliminary negotiations continued throughout 1948.

In February, 1949, ECA's report stated that arrangements for tin purchases were "proceeding smoothly" and that "preliminary work for the preparation of tin samples for shipment to the U.S." had "been completed."[12] All of the transactions were conducted between ECA and private companies even though the Nationalist government's Natural Resources Commission objected. NRC felt these arrangements should be made government to government with public interests taking precedence over private.[13] In spite of this, ECA representatives continued to deal with privately owned businesses. The Yunnan Consolidated Tin Corporation, the Nanyang Finance Development Corporation and T.K. Li and Company were three firms engaged in investigating and negotiating the procurement of tin for the United States.[14]

On June 1, 1949, when the departure of ECA's leaders was imminent, an American agency agreed to accept up to three hundred tons of tin under a contract with the Yunnan Consolidated Tin Corporation. At the same time, ECA notified the agency it could no longer help with tin contracts and recommended that future arrangements be made directly between the agency and the sellers in China.[15]

Except for direct acquisition of tin, no tangible results were realized from this part of the aid program. As Roger Lapham summed it up:

We had planned to spend money for a Reconstruction and Replacement program — rebuilding railroads, building additional power plants, modernizing coal mines, and for various other very necessary projects in different parts of China. Practically none of the funds allocated for this purpose were spent, when it became apparent that the Communists were likely to occupy most of China by the time any work could be started, let alone completed.[16]

RURAL RECONSTRUCTION

The Joint Commission on Rural Reconstruction which began its work in China in 1948 carried on where UNRRA and another aid effort, the Agricultural Industry Service, left off. Both of these agencies had emphasized a technological approach to solving China's agricultural problems, an emphasis that rested on improvement of farming techniques.[17] China needed to have the advantage of the newest methods to improve its farm production, but, as JCRR eventually learned, there were other problems which had to be solved first.

The idea of giving help to China's agriculture industry through the China Aid Act began when Dr. Y. C. James Yen, head of the Mass Education Movement, came to the United States to try to persuade the American government to give extensive assistance to a program of rural reconstruction in China.[18]

Yen, a well-known Chinese educator, had been involved for years in projects to help his country's peasant population. During World War I, he had been an interpreter in France with a Chinese labor corps. The men in the group were poor farm boys who, because of their inability to read and write, were completely cut off from their friends and families in China. Yen tried to teach them but, although they proved to be eager to learn, the difficulty of the classical language made it almost impossible. Determined to find a way to help these men, he decided to teach them only the characters in their vocabulary, thereby reducing the number of ideographs to one thousand. This proved so successful that Yen continued his work on his return to China and began what came to be known as the Mass Education Movement.[19]

In 1927, the movement became not only a literacy campaign but a program to improve the lives of China's peasants in other ways. Many rural reconstruction projects were initiated involving reform of local governments, health programs, and improved agricultural methods.

Dr. Yen's expertise in this field was widely known and he came to Washington as a respected and informed petitioner for American aid.

In talks with Secretary of State Marshall and President Truman, Dr. Yen said that "the economic and social front was just as important as the military front, that the rice field was even more vital than the battlefield."[20] In a memorandum for the President, Yen suggested that 10 per cent of the proposed aid to China be allotted for rural reconstruction. According to one author, "President Truman was impressed with the practical and fundamental nature of the proposal and supported it heartily."[21] The idea won the approval of many members of Congress as well, and the aid bill was subsequently set up with the recommended allocation for rural assistance.

After an exchange of notes between the governments of the United States and China, the Joint Commission was set up in August, 1948. The three Chinese members of the commission appointed the same month were Dr. Chiang Mon-lin, former Chancellor of Peking University, Chairman; Dr. T. H. Shen, agricultural expert; and the man whose suggestions had been so well-received in Washington, Dr. Y. C. James Yen. In September, President Truman appointed two Americans, Dr. Raymond T. Moyer, an authority on Chinese agriculture, and Dr. John Earl Baker, economic adviser to the nationalist government periodically since 1916 and a man who for over thirty years had been involved with American aid and relief missions to China.[22]

The first meeting of the commission was held on October 1, 1948. Dr. Chiang Mon-lin was elected chairman, and as he said later, "In the throes of idealogical (sic) confusion, economic chaos, social discontentment, political turmoil, and military reverses, the Joint Commission set sail on rough seas."[23] In November, after weeks of intensive study in Nanking, members of the commission made trips throughout the areas where aid money was to be spent. They visited Chungking, Chengtu, and Changsha, with side trips out of Chungking to Pehpei and Pishan where James Yen's Mass Education Movement had had good results. According to the Monthly report, the commission's program was to be divided into four areas. First and most important, they wanted to increase agricultural production. Second, they wished to aid government agencies in order to improve "local government administration, land reform, agriculture, health, and social education." Third, they wanted to initiate education programs for the farm population to "enable them to participate more intelligently in solving their . . . problems." Fourth, they intended to provide assistance to reconstruction projects initiated locally by private or government agencies.[24]

JCRR was divided administratively into seven divisions, each centered around part of the program, such as irrigation, rural health, education, visual aids, etc. The visual aids section used posters and other illustrated materials to get messages across to a largely illiterate population. For example, one poster illustrated the importance of the inoculation of cattle against disease.[25] This section of JCRR also labeled aid goods so the people who were the recipients would be aware of their benefactors. Frequently, the message was "The United States Government and people have contributed their money to this cause."[26]

JCRR's main office was in Nanking with regional offices in Chungking, Szechuan; Changsha, Hunan; Kweilin, Kwangsi; and Canton, Kwangtung. Communist victories in the fall of 1948 prevented opening two offices planned for North China.[27] The regional offices helped select and supervise field operations and also kept in touch with research institutes, universities and colleges, and local officials.

In an attempt to avoid the pitfalls of inflation encountered by all other agencies of ECA, JCRR decided to pay its share on an installment basis. The local agency was required to pay the first 10 per cent whereupon JCRR would pay its first installment. This alternating payment plan kept the inflationary effect at a minimum.[28]

In spite of the war and Communist advances, which interrupted some projects almost before they were started, several important programs were successfully implemented. By January, 1949, extensive work had been done on dike repairs in Hunan province. Tung T'ing Lake which served as a reservoir for five rivers, had had its dikes broken the preceding spring when torrential rains flooded the rivers. The subsequent inundation of the surrounding land caused this "to become the primary economic problem of Hunan province, and Governor Cheng Chien approached JCRR for assistance to prevent the recurrence of a similar disaster this spring."[29] The flooded area was known as China's "rice bowl" and was the prewar source of most of the rice for Shanghai as well as the supply for the province's population of over 1,000,000.

Hunan was also chosen as the area where JCRR planned to help establish producer's cooperatives. Only tenant farmers were eligible to join and the cooperatives were planned to help them collect rents and pay landowners, ensure that landowners did not evict them unfairly,

prevent unjust rent increases, loan funds to peasants for land purchases, and buy land for cooperative use.[30] This project was not implemented throughout the province, but it represents one of JCRR's
efforts to experiment with land reform. Several months were to pass,
however, before the commissioners became convinced that land reform was the vital cornerstone of agricultural improvement in China.

Meanwhile, JCRR continued to work on its many other projects.
According to a statement made by Dr. Chiang Mon-lin, these projects
had been selected on the basis of the personal inspection trips by
commission members and by investigation of the more than four
hundred requests for assistance from almost every province in the
country.[31] Education of the farm population was one of the
commission's favorite objectives. Reading was taught using the "Tao
Sheng" method where a person who could read taught his neighbors.
Reading materials were paid for out of JCRR funds and provided
information in health, sanitation, and new agricultural techniques.
Other projects gave assistance to weaving cooperatives which had been
set up earlier, began construction of 2,000 small irrigation ponds to
hold back stream water, advanced money for purchase of 1,000 water
buffalo, started several reforestation projects, and distributed 10,000
pounds of improved rice and wheat seeds.[32]

During the winter of 1948-49, a pilot program was begun which
showed promise of lending assistance of a different kind to a rural area
of China. An American survey group traveled to the Northwest to
investigate the possibility of re-establishing the area's rug-making industries. A report written by a member of the group described the
initiation of such a project in the city of Ching-t'ai, located south of the
Great Wall near the Alashan mountains. The town itself was remote
and as the report stated:

> Ching-t'ai probably won't make Hollywood. No travel agency will ever
> include it within its prospectus; it boasts no sacred nor historical spots. It
> is nothing but a small, walled, one-time (Ming Dyn)* garrision post
> situated within the periphery of the Alashan sand dunes but politically
> within the confines of Kansu province.[33] [* Ming Dynasty, 1366-1644.]

The road to the city was a "narrow, maze-like strip of finely pow-
dered dust twisting its way between sand dunes and the jagged wind-
swept rocks." The countryside, though appearing barren, was thought
to be rich in natural resources untapped by the 30,000 to 40,000 people

who lived there. They were "like a child starving in the midst of tinned food he didn't know how to open." The few raw materials they utilized were processed in a very rudimentary manner.

> The mining methods are very primitive: cotton thread is spun by the whorl method, the cotton having been de-seeded by a blind-folded donkey-power-jin. Wool has always been shipped to Lanchow, about 180 kilometers away, where it is washed, sorted, and packed for Western markets. There is almost no industry within the area. The people seem to have been in the rut of lethargy for hundreds of years.[34]

During its short period in Ching-t'ai, ECA occupied the "largest installation in town, a courtyard with 41 chien of buildings (formerly housing the local garrison) for offices, rug factory, and workers quarters." The Americans purchased equipment from a defunct rug-making business and began a training program. When the industry had been prominent in the area, rug-making had been a man's profession. Forced conscription had diminished their ranks, however, and those who were not in the army had run away. ECA representatives hoped eventually to persuade those who heard of the new project to come out of hiding, but, in the meantime, the training program would begin to provide the necessary skilled personnel. When ECA leaders discovered that "eye diseases are so prevalent that the people consider them natural," they set up a medical program as well.

The author of the report on Ching-t'ai was very enthusiastic about the potential benefits of American aid, not only as an economic boon to the area, but as an opportunity to influence people in what might be a strategically sensitive section of the country. As the report pointed out:

> Being in the Kansu corridor the people seem to be aware of the imminence of Russia. During the war many Russians came into Kansu and especially Lanchou. Apparently Russia has done nothing for nor given anything to any people here. The Central Gov't has done no more. The U.S. with no previous fanfare (we arrived so suddenly that no one even had time to hike prices) has come with a plan to stimulate immediately some economic activity.[35]

Although projects in the Northwest were mentioned in JCRR plans later in 1949,[36] it is not known if aid continued to go to Ching-t'ai after the first part of the year. The program is significant, however, as an illustration of the diverse interest and endeavors of the aid mission.*

* Another example of ECA's diverse interests was a long overdue dredging of the Pearl River channel called Elliot Reach. Work on the project began in July, 1948, and by

One of the most significant changes in aid to rural reconstruction developed slowly throughout the year. With few exceptions, ECA's rural programs were superimposed on the already existing landlord-tenant structure of China's agricultural industry. As the months passed, the commissioners began to realize that before the farmers could benefit from the technological improvements the agronomists could impart to them, the land itself would have to be more equitably distributed.[37]

In April, 1949, Paul H. Johnstone, an economist with ECA, wrote a memorandum recommending that the mission begin to emphasize land reform projects. Noting that the "political strength of the Communists has been built on the foundation of their espousal of the cause of land reform," he felt that, "opposition to Communism has in large measure lost out by defaulting on this issue." Redistribution, it seemed to Johnstone, was long overdue and

> If an American aid effort devoted itself . . . to assisting in land reform, it would be working with the tide instead of against it. We would at the same time accomplish much good, . . . and associate America with a movement that is irrepressible and of vast popularity.[38]

Allen Griffin lent his support to the idea as well. In a statement made just before he left China in June, he noted that JCRR would be the only ECA program to continue to operate on the mainland. "This is the last, though perhaps the most important, effort of American Aid." He pointed out that

> The job of JCRR is more than building dykes, supporting irrigation projects, or the improvement of seeds and control of animal and human diseases. The great aim of JCRR must be to assure that the benefits of

---

January, 1949, large river boats were able to go upriver directly to the city of Canton. According to the ECA report, the channel had been blocked since the Opium War "more than a century ago when the Chinese sank junks filled with rock in the passage in order to prevent British frigates from reaching Canton. Timber piles were driven to reinforce the barrier." Tremendous shipping costs after World War II were the impetus for ECA's dredging project. "At times, freight charges from the United States to Canton were less than rates from Whampoa to Canton." *ECA Monthly Report, No. 5* (January, 1949), Griffin Papers. In addition to the clearing of the channel, the February report listed repairs to the Shanghai Seawall, dike reconstruction near Hangchow, culvert building along the Yangtze River, replacement of sections of the Kiangsu Seawall, and construction of the Liangkam Dam in Kwangtung. *ECA Monthly Report, No. 6* (February, 1949), Griffin Papers. It is not known if any projects, other than the Elliot Reach dredging, were completed.

increased production go more and more to the peasant producer and that the abuses that have laid a heavy hand upon the Chinese farmer are stopped. JCRR must push the land reform that has been talked about so much but about which so little has been accomplished.[39]

Commission leaders apparently agreed with Johnstone and Griffin and, according to one author, at a meeting in June, 1949, finally decided to try to shift JCRR's emphasis to deal with land reform.[40] Their decision came too late, however, to have an effect on the mainland.*

After Roger Lapham and Allen Griffin left China, and other ECA programs were discontinued, JCRR was set up as a separate agency. Dr. Raymond Moyer was appointed Special ECA Representative to supervise the programs. Most of the rural projects which continued in force were similar to those previously undertaken and land reform received only minor attention. In June, a detailed list of JCRR's planned activities included the usual emphasis on distribution of improved rice seeds, irrigation and drainage projects, cattle vaccination, dispersal of fertilizers and pesticides, adult education and public health.[41] All the projects were to be short-lived, however, for the Communists consolidated their position in the southern provinces in the summer and fall, and JCRR moved its headquarters to Taiwan.

During its year on the mainland, the rural reconstruction program emerged in the minds of ECA's leaders as the most significant of all the mission's efforts. In March, 1949, when Roger Lapham was in Washington to make known his recommendations on additional aid to China, he stressed the importance of JCRR. He had come to feel that any future aid should be concentrated in rural not urban areas where the United States would have the opportunity to reach China's vast peasant population. In a memorandum to Paul Hoffman he wrote:

> Let us lead as many Chinese as we can along the lines proposed by the JCRR — Land conservancy, improved agricultural methods, medical and sanitary instruction, schools for children and adults, mass education. Let us by our actions develop counter-propaganda to offset distorted Communist propaganda.[42]

Again in September, 1949, Lapham and Allen Griffin made similar recommendations. They had been requested to express their views on

*One of the first problems JCRR tried to solve on Taiwan, however, was the redistribution of land.

China by Ambassador-at-Large Philip C. Jessup. The Ambassador sought information from many people who had had experience in the country for a conference on China policy to be held in Washington in October, 1949. The paper submitted by Lapham and Griffin emphasized the importance of continued contact with the Chinese Communist government, especially through JCRR projects.

> Means should be provided whereby U.S. Government financed assistance could be funneled to appropriate American supervised organizations to carry on this type of work, and every effort made to induce the Sino-Communists to accept such assistance under American supervision.[43]

It is unlikely the Communists would have agreed to American involvement in their rural projects, but this memorandum clearly reflected the confidence mission leaders had acquired in the efforts of JCRR.

Writing several months later to a friend, Roger Lapham expressed regret that the potential of rural aid had not been realized earlier:

> I have had a great deal more time to think things over than I had while in China, where we had to make minute-to-minute decisions and spent much of our time planning where and how to move to the next place. Looking backward now, I am thoroughly convinced that the JCRR type of organization was the best vehicle we had to put over pro-USA propaganda. It's a shame we didn't work along these lines beginning right after V-J Day. Certainly it would have cost us much less and we would have been reaching the country instead of a few larger cities in which ECA operated.[44]

Although JCRR projects were not given the priority Lapham retrospectively would have bestowed on them, they were among the most helpful to China's people. The need was so great, however, that the few million dollars spent by ECA had very little long-lasting effect. The country's basic problems with the economy and the war were not solved, and ECA had been unable to provide either a "respite" or a "stay of execution" for the Nationalists. The Truman administration's policy of limited assistance, which the mission represented, failed to have a significant effect in China.

In the United States, the concomitant goal the policy was designed to fulfill also proved ineffectual; Republican critics were not quieted. Thoughout the year the ECA operated on the mainland, the Congressional China bloc and other supporters of Chiang Kai-shek continued their barrage. Instead of being quieted by Truman's re-election in November, 1948, their attack persisted and accelerated.

Ironically, the very men who had been chosen to carry out the administration's China policy disagreed with leaders in Washington. From the beginning of their mission, Roger Lapham, Allen Griffin, and other ECA representatives often were not in accord with the State Department. They recommended changes, and questioned policy in general. Although they were dedicated to the basic American goal of trying to halt world communism, their methods for handling the problem in Asia differed from the ones they were assigned to China to try to carry out.

Chapter 6 Footnotes

[1] Harlan Cleveland, "Economic Aid to China," *Far Eastern Survey*, XVIII (January 12, 1949), 4.

[2] Dorothy Borg, "ECA and US Policy in China," *Far Eastern Survey*, XVIII (August 24, 1949), 199.

[3] *China White Paper*, II, 1031.

[4] News conference reported in *Chinese News Service*, September 1, 1948.

[5] *Ibid.*

[6] Harlan Cleveland, "Economic Aid to China," *Far Eastern Survey*, XVIII (January 12, 1949), 4.

[7] *ECA Monthly Report, No. 2* (October, 1948), Griffin Papers. For further information, see *China White Paper, II*, 1033-34.

[8] *ECA Monthly Report, No. 2* (October, 1948), Griffin Papers.

[9] *China White Paper*, I, 401.

[10] Negotiations for tin had gone on with China for many years. See Arthur N. Young. *China and the Helping Hand, 1937-1945* (Cambridge, Massachusetts: Harvard University Press, 1963), pp. 132, 209, 294, 326.

[11] *China White Paper*, II, 1039.

[12] *ECA Monthly Report, No. 6* (Februrary, 1949), Griffin Papers.

[13] Dorothy Borg, "ECA and US Policy in China," *Far Eastern Survey*, XVIII (August 24, 1949), 200.

[14] *ECA Monthly Report, No. 6* (February, 1949), Griffin Paper.

[15] Two telegrams to the American Consul in Kunming dated June 1, 1949, from R. Allen Griffin. Griffin Papers.

[16] Address by Roger Lapham to the Commonwealth Club of California, San Francisco, California, September 8, 1949. "The Chinese Situation As I Saw It." Copy in Griffin Papers.

[17] Melvin Conant, Jr., "JCRR: An Object Lesson," *Far Eastern Survey*, XX (May, 1951), 88.

[18] Gerard Swope and Richard J. Walsh, "Mass Education Movement and JCRR," *Far Eastern Survey*, XX (July 25, 1951), 147.

[19] C.P. Fitzgerald, *The Birth of Communist China*, pp. 158-59.

[20] Gerald Swope and Richard J. Walsh, "Mass Education Movement and JCRR," *Far Eastern Survey*, XX (July 25, 1951), 147.

[21] *Ibid.*, p. 148.

[22] *China White Paper*, II, 1035.

[23] John D. Montgomery, Rufus B. Hughes, Raymond H. Davis, *Rural Improvement and Political Development: The JCRR Model* (Washington, D.C.: Comparative Administration Group, American Society for Public Administration, 1966), p. 8.

[24] *ECA Monthly Report, No. 3* (November, 1948), Griffin Papers.

[25] Many of the posters are in the Griffin Papers.

[26] Melvin Conant, Jr., "JCRR: An Object Lesson," *Far Eastern Survey*, XX (May 2, 1951), 91.

[27] *China White Paper*, II, 1037.

[28] Melvin Conant, Jr. "JCRR: An Object Lesson," *Far Eastern Survey*, XX (May 2, 1951), 91.

[29] *ECA Monthly Report, No. 5* (January, 1949), Griffin Papers.

[30] *Ibid.*

[31] *ECA Monthly Report, No. 6* (February, 1949), Griffin Papers.

[32] *Ibid.*

[33] *Report from Northwest for Week Ending 6 March, 1949. Griffin Papers.*

[34] *Ibid.*

[35] *Ibid.*

[36] *Joint Commission on Rural Reconstruction*, June 23, 1949. Griffin Papers.

[37] John D. Montogmery and others, *Rural Improvement and Political Development: The JCRR Model*, p. 9.

[38] Memorandum to R. Allen Griffin and Norman J. Meiklejohn from Paul H. Johnstone, entitled "Observations Concerning Potentialities of JCRR Program in Kwangsi," dated April 7, 1949. Griffin Papers.

[39] Statement by R. Allen Griffin, Hong Kong, June 6, 1949. Griffin Papers.

[40] Melvin Conant, Jr., "JCRR: An Object Lesson," *Far Eastern Survey*, XX (May 2, 1951), 90.

[41] *Joint Commission on Rural Reconstruction*, June 23, 1949. Griffin Papers.

[42] Memorandum to Paul G. Hoffman from Roger Lapham, entitled "Recommendations re China Policy," dated March 9, 1949. Griffin Papers.

[43] Memorandum to Ambassdor-at-Large Philip C. Jessup from Roger Lapham and R. Allen Griffin, dated September 19, 1949. Griffin Papers.

[44] Letter to H. Medill Sarkisian from Roger Lapham, dated January 27, 1950. Griffin Papers.

ECA Policy Recommendations

The primary concern of American policy makers throughout 1948 was the increasingly threatening situation in Europe. Early in the year a Communist coup had overthrown the government of Czechoslovakia; a government which under President Eduard Benes had tried to remain neutral in the Cold War. Evidence of Russian involvement in the coup seemed to Western leaders to indicate that the Soviet Union was continuing to carry out a plan for world conquest. Three months later these suspicions were further enforced when, in an attempt to block American plans for currency reform and formulation of a new government for West Germany, the Soviet Union began a blockade of Berlin. America's response, an air lift of food and supplies for the city which continued from June, 1948, to May, 1949, helped focus the attention of American policy makers on Europe where the drama of the blockade seemed closer and more threatening than the drama unfolding in Asia.

The Truman administration met the challenge of the Soviet Union with the air lift, with implementation of the Marshall Plan, with increased negotiations for military alliances, and with urgings for universal military training. On the other hand, China's portion for the Cold War amounted to the funds for ECA and a military grant of $125,000,000. The latter was to be used as the Nationalist government saw fit and was not under the jurisdiction of ECA. ECA, however, which had not been set up as a policy making organization and which had no control over military aid began to proffer advice on the expenditure of the military aid funds.

This unsolicited counsel did not meet with approval in Washington, and represented the first of four major issues in which ECA personnel were involved in recommending policy which was antithetic to State Department wishes. In each case, with George Marshall as Secretary of State until December, 1948, and with Dean Acheson in the position from January, 1949, to the end of the mission in June, the ECA recommendations were overruled by opposing State Department opinion. Although ECA was not under the direct jurisdiction of State, the

Department's advice carried more weight with the President and in the ensuing controversies, Truman's decisions were in line with State Department proposals.

The opposing views of the two government agencies were foreshadowed early in the mission when ECA leaders requested an outline of America's long-range plans for China policy. In a memorandum in July, 1948, Harlan Cleveland noted that "The present program was conceived, and is generally recognized, as a finger-in-the-dike proposition." [1] It seemed important to him, therefore, to think beyond the next few months, and he urged policy makers to formulate and make known their long-range plans. Some of the questions he hoped would be answered by such a projection were set forth in a September memo.

> What strategic objectives in the Far East should United States aid to China be designed to support? Where should our aid be concentrated? What kinds of aid are likely to be most effective? What political and economic relationships among the countries of the Far East should United States economic aid be designed to support? What kinds of economic aid are called for in order to achieve this pattern? [2]

A meeting with W. Walton Butterworth, Head of the Far Eastern Desk, however, revealed that the State Department would be very unlikely to support long-range planning with the situation in Asia in such a state of flux. Butterworth said that it was his "own view that no advance planning would be of much assistance in dealing with the China situation." As far as Secretary Marshall was concerned, Butterworth "thought it highly unlikely that the Secretary would change the position he had consistently taken, particularly the strong desire not to get involved in Chinese affairs too deeply or to get committed to direct support of the Chinese Government's military effort." In the discussion, ECA representatives, who "dissented rather vigorously from this negative line of argument, . . . received the strong impression that it was a position that would not be lightly abandoned." Cleveland's own conclusion was that ECA should "develop some sensible proposals" with the military services and should keep State informed, but not expect them to take the initiative. [3]

This apparent lack of long-range planning by State was a source of bewilderment and irritation to ECA leaders throughout their mission. They were also disturbed by the lack of high level coordination between American representatives in China. As Cleveland wrote to Paul Hoffman, "The only means of coordination is the informal . . . liaison established by Mr. Lapham with the Embassy and with the United States military missions." [4] A discussion with Butterworth, however, revealed that he felt that "coordination of such planning on the part of American agencies in the field was not particularly important since the foreign policy decisions had to be reached in Washington anyway." [5]

This view did not prove acceptable to Roger Lapham and other representatives in China and they tried to set forth a consistent and coordinated American policy. It was out of this effort that an alternative plan for military aid emerged.

REGIONAL AID

A few weeks after he arrived in Shanghai, Roger Lapham traveled through North China with Admiral Oscar C. Badger,* and Ambassador Stuart.[6] The three men agreed that alternatives should be sought for distribution of American aid. They were disillusioned with Chiang Kai-shek's leadership, his lack of effort toward reforms of his government, and his conduct of the war.[7] In September, Roger Lapham wrote Paul Hoffman complaining that, "We here who are trying to maintain the Nationalist Government, which today is the only one we could look to, are dreadfully handicapped by the incompetence of that Government and that is putting it mildly." [8]

It is not known which of the three men, Lapham, Badger, or Stuart, first concluded that the United States might consider by-passing the Generalissimo by directing aid to regional leaders. A year earlier, however, Ambassador Stuart had recommended that Chiang allow local leaders greater independent action. After a trip to Peking in July, 1947, he reported to the State Department that he had told China's President "that it was my strong opinion that reliance on trusted local leaders with a large measure of autonomy would strengthen the Government position and neutralize Communist success in using these same methods." [9] In March, 1948, in another report to the department, he noted that there was a "new growth of regionalism," caused by

---

* Admiral Oscar C. Badger was a third generation Navy man who graduated from the Naval Academy in 1911. He was the Commander of the United States Naval Forces in the Far East and had been appointed to the post in February, 1948. (*Current Biography, Who's News and Why, 1949* [New York: The H. H. Wilson Company, 1951], pp. 16-18.)

Chiang's weak and inept leadership. Many Chinese officials "believe that the time has come when they must look to their own interests as a matter of self preservation, and are so proceeding to develop a direct and personal control in regions where they are assigned." [10] The Ambassador mentioned Dr. T. V. Soong in South China and General Fu Tso-yi in North China. General Fu's increasing independence from the central government was again noted in a report to the State Department in May, [11] and a July report revealed that, "From information available to us, it appears that, with the exception of Fu Tso-yi, Nationalist commanders are avoiding combat and are abandoning their positions when combat threatens." [12]

Out of these observations by American officials, a plan grew to try to give American military aid directly to General Fu Tso-yi. This plan was apparently formulated after Lapham, Badger, and Stuart traveled to North China in July, 1948, to see for themselves if what they had heard about the General was true. Fu was not a member of Chiang Kai-shek's favored clique of officers from the Nationalist Military Academy at Whampoa. He was a native of Shansi in North China and had served in the army of Governor Yen Hsi-shan, known as the "Model Governor." In 1928, Fu had valiantly defended the small city of Chochow in a siege. Again in 1936, when most Nationalist armies seemed to be losing to the Japanese, the General won national acclaim with his actions against enemy forces in Mongolia. In 1948, when he came to the attention of American leaders in China, he had been given command of Peking and Tientsin by Chiang Kai-shek. As historian C. P. Fitzgerald pointed out, however, this was not a position reflecting the Generalissimo's confidence in Fu, but rather an indication of the government's growing weakness. When the Nationalists had been stronger, the General's capabilities as a military leader had not been rewarded with an important command. [13]

On July 28, 1948, mission leaders met with General Fu Tso-yi at the Summer Palace outside of Peking. The General said he hoped to receive small arms and ammunition for his one hundred thousand trained and disciplined troops. China's Vice-President, Li Tsung-jen, in a meeting the same day "expressed confidence in the strength of resistance in North China" and recommended that American aid be sent to the area. In a subsequent meeting on July 31, Li set forth a somewhat stronger argument on behalf of General Fu. The Vice-

President criticized "the position of the Nanking government toward North China and . . . the military policies of the Generalissimo." He suggested that American aid would keep certain areas relatively strong and that after a collapse, a new central government could "knit together" the regional governments and armies. The Vice President still hoped that Chiang Kai-shek would begin to understand the problems and take the necessary steps to alter the desperate situation, but "he failed to express any belief that such a change was probable."[13a]

After the meetings, the Americans agreed that General Fu Tso-yi seemed an able leader and a deserving recipient of aid. Roger Lapham called him the "one White Hope in North China."[14] Admiral Badger felt that the General would make good use of any military supplies the United States was able to send to him and indicated in a meeting with mission leaders on August 5, 1948, "that he felt it a matter of great necessity that General Fu Tso-yi receive the modest amount of military supplies that he required to complete the arming of his troops and to maintain an armed militia." In order to expedite this, the Admiral had already ordered small arms "for 120,000 men (100,000 for North China, 20,000 for Tsingtao) to be shipped to his custody from Guam." He said he expected to have the armament in his possession in ten days and with an expedient financial settlement, he could deliver the material to the troops in twenty-four hours. Badger went on to say that "he was acting with the approval and under the authority of the Joint Chiefs of Staff and that he felt emphatically that 'we' must be prepared to safeguard United States interests in North China as a barrier."[14a]*

In later testimony, Badger recalled the visit to the Northern leader:

> We talked to Fu Tso-yi, inspected Fu Tso-yi's armies; we visited the villages, we pretty well covered that part of North China; and as a result of that visit we sent a joint recommendation to Washington, the Joint Chiefs of Staff, recommending that specific support be given to Fu Tso-yi.[15]

The Admiral also made his wishes known in a personal letter to Secretary of Defense James V. Forrestal wherein he described General Fu's armies as "very impressive in their appearance, actions, and spirit.

---

* Admiral Badger's plans to acquire and disperse arms to North China were never carried out, and in an October meeting with Lapham and Griffin he expressed his bitter disappointment that the entire arms deal had been taken out of his jurisdiction and turned over to the Army. Notes of Meeting, October 9, 1948. Griffin Papers.

Their loyalty to General Fu was unmistakably of the highest degree." [16] Their need for ammunition and equipment seemed to be what prevented them from being an effective force against the Communists, according to Badger; he hoped the American leaders would be willing to send Fu a portion of the military aid allotted to the Nationalists. Badger's testimony emphasized that the recommendation of aid for Fu was not seen as a panacea for the country's military problems, but was an alternative plan which might work:

> Don't misunderstand me . . . I don't mean to say that we were able to say that this aid would have meant the difference between success and failure; but it was stated by those authoritative people, and not by me as an individual . . . that it was a pretty darned favorable background for success, and . . . gave promise of what we considered to be better than 50-50.[17]

Admiral Badger asked General Fu for a list of the supplies needed by his armies; a list which the Admiral subsequently sent to the Army advisory group in China, the Ambassador, the Joint Chiefs of Staff, all of whom approved.

Roger Lapham felt the plan to send American aid to Fu Tso-yi might be a successful means of retarding the progress of the Communists. When they arrived in June, he and other ECA officials were shocked by conditions in the country. They noted in a July report that "The mission was really startled by the facts about the military situation in China and to find such an enormous gap between what they had supposed to be the case and the actual truth." [18] Allen Griffin said later that he had been in China only a week when he knew that Chiang Kai-shek would lose the War.[19] Under the circumstances, the plan to help General Fu seemed to ECA officials a viable strategic alternative. Their growing interest in the plan was reflected in Harlan Cleveland's reports. In a July memorandum, he reported the trend toward political fragmentation and growth of regional governments. He said the leaders in North China felt they had been abandoned by the central government.[20] In a similar memorandum a month later, Cleveland reported that the move toward regionalism was growing and although the Nationalist government was neglecting North China, American officials in the country felt the United States could not "afford to write off the North" and the "logic of United States interests in China requires that an important part of American aid be used in the critical area of North China." According to the memo, American leaders hoped to get aid to Fu Tso-yi and other northern army commanders and to that end, "Admiral Badger in Tsingtao is stockpiling arms and ammunition, pending approval to turn it over directly to the Chinese military in the North."[21]

While they awaited the arrival of additional military aid for regional leaders, Stuart, Badger, and Lapham learned that their plan had been seriously questioned in Washington. The Army and State Department's assessment of the situation did not coincide with that of the American representatives in China. The first indication that support for regional commanders might be challenged came in a letter to Paul Hoffman from the Secretary of the Army, Kenneth C. Royall. The Secretary reminded Hoffman of a briefing Army Department officers had given to him and to Lapham and Stillman on the military situation in North China. They had been told that conditions were "unstable, and, from the point of view of the Nationalist Government of China, . . . very unsatisfactory." Based on this, Royall reminded Hoffman, the Army had recommended that all future American efforts should go to South China, where the Communists would be less likely to take over the supplies or to benefit from them. He had heard, the Secretary's letter went on, that ECA officials had gone to North China and had reported that the military situation was not as bad as the earlier Army Department information had indicated. As a result, on the 24th of September, Army personnel had reinvestigated and found the situation to be the same as in their earlier report. In a meeting a few days later, Secretary Royall and Under Secretary of State Robert Lovett outlined to Hoffman the Army's latest intelligence assessment of the China situation:* 1. In Manchuria, the Communists would probably capture Changchun by spring and the Nationalists would probably continue to hold Mukden. 2. In North China, the Communists would "retain the initiative in rural areas, developing an area base for Central China operations, and attack secondary cities." 3. Fu Tso-yi's military abilities were "likely to decline," and although American equipment

---

* Apparently this report was not sent to Admiral Badger who felt he should have been advised since he was the ranking American military man in China and would, in the event of war involving the United States, "take command of operations in this theater automatically." To Roger Lapham from R. Allen Griffin, October 9, 1948. Roger D. Lapham Papers, Hoover Institution on War, Revolution and Peace, Stanford, California.

might help him defend his positions for a short time, it would not in the long run stop the Communists. 4. Without a major change in the military situation, ECA should not use funds in North China or Manchuria. 5. If any aid were given to the North, it should only go to cities to maintain the "economy and morale*." [22]

A few days after Secretary Royall presented the Army's position, Hoffman received a phone call from Robert Lovett in which he explained that the State Department agreed with the Army on the matter of North China. [23] On October 1, 1948, Lapham received cabled instructions from Paul Hoffman to hold all commitments to North China and Manchuria "in view of seriousness of the situation and also of formal warnings given me by both Army and State." [24]

Since the State Department did not have direct jurisdiction over ECA, however, the issue was not immediately resolved, and ECA officials continued to present their side of the case in their communications with Washington. Lapham cabled Hoffman, "Still hold personal convictions our own national interest calls for support North China not only moral but material." [25] In a letter written a few days later, Allen Griffin informed the Deputy Director of Army Intelligence, Major General A. R. Bolling that:

> In the course of our operations here we do everything that is possible under the law to render assistance in areas affected by military operations. In some instances, this is an important morale factor, and in some instances, it is a factor in production for military uses. In short, the purpose of this Mission, as interpreted by its Chief and as enthusiastically espoused by myself, is to back up U.S. military policy as much as we possibly can. . . . Recently a letter of the Secretary of the Army to Mr. Hoffman, Administrator of ECA, caused a sudden flurry of panic among some of our associates in Washington. This was accompanied also by a reiterated reluctance of some other agencies in Washington to give any support to China that is more effective than pouring American money down a rat hole. Fortunately, in the copy of these communications that I received was your estimate of the situation, that was followed or accompanied by your second memorandum of 24 September, 1948, to General Wedemeyer in which you outlined your thoughts on projects designed to accomplish two essential things: "Maintain a working economy in the area" and "maintain morale of the local populace."

---

* As it turned out, the Army Report was too optimistic. By the end of October both Changchun and Mukden had fallen to the Communists and three months both Peking and Tientsin were also lost by the Nationalists.

Frankly, General Bolling, that helped take the curse off some of the suggestions from Washington that we stop cooperating for the purpose of sustaining, . . . the area that is commanded by China's apparently most able commander, General Fu Tso-yi.[26]

Griffin went on to thank General Bolling for backing up ECA in the situation. Actually, Griffin may have read too much into Bolling's memos since assistance to North China's economy and morale could be quite different from military assistance to General Fu Tso-yi. Nevertheless, the letter further illustrates the confidence ECA leaders continued to place in the plan for regional aid.

Charles Stillman who called the issue a "pretty hot potato" which he hoped would "burn somebody but us," [27] wrote a lengthy memorandum to Paul Hoffman early in October in which he outlined what he considered to be the unanimous opinion of ECA officials, Admiral Badger, and Ambassador Stuart.

1. No exception is taken to the estimate of the situation as stated by the Army in their letter to you — unless steps are taken to change the situation . . .

2. We do not believe that such an estimate should . . . be accepted supinely as something about which nothing will be done by ECA or by other agencies of the United States.

3. For example, it should be noted that as of this date, no arms or ammunition have been shipped to China under the military aid program of the China Aid Act of 1948 although more than six months have passed since the passage of the act. In fact, there are not, as yet, any prices for arms to be supplied out of U.S. military stocks despite persistent emphatic requests by Admiral Badger . . .

4. The Army Advisory Group in Nanking are apparently charged with the development of a peacetime military establishment for the defense of China. They seem to be inhibited from giving advice on the conduct of the war or from taking any responsibility for the outcome of such advice as they may proffer . . .

5. Reference is hereby made to the cables filed over the past six or seven months by Admiral Badger to the Joint Chiefs of Staff. This source would develop the opinions and efforts of the Admiral to obtain military assistance to reverse or hold in check the further deterioration of the North China military situation and its paramount importance to the U.S. military policy as established by the Joint Chiefs of Staff. This was to be accomplished through the assistance pursuant to the military portion of the China Aid Act of 1948 for the armies under the command of General Fu Tso-yi and to strengthen the Nationalist forces at Tsingtao.

Stillman further pointed out that American officials in China had made their policy recommendations because the legislation under which they operated and were obliged to "observe was designed as a holding operation to aid a country engaged in a life and death struggle against the 'Iron Curtain' — i.e., potential enemies of the United States." In the judgment of "the Senior military officer of the United States, representing the Joint Chiefs of Staff," the Ambassador and ECA officials, the policy of support to regional leaders was the best means to carry out the mission for which they had been sent to China. They did not feel that aid to South China alone was the correct solution.

> We do not consider it economically feasible for a government controlling only South China to maintain armies and to continue to offer effective resistance to the spread of Communism or to the fragmentation of the Country. If Nationalist China is confined south of the Yangtze and North China is in the hands of the Communists, it will surely cause great change in the U. S. foreign policy . . . No program of Reconstruction and Replacement can be built on the bland assumption that after North China is gone the interests of the United States will simply fall back to South China . . . In summary and on the basis of the foregoing, I can only hope that the interpretation which you placed at first glance on the Army letter is one which will be clarified as an endorsement of our program. If, on the other hand, the Army should confirm that it seeks to advise ECA to modify its program to conform to a fatalistic estimate of the military situation, such advice should be rejected as not being in the best interests of the United States, as contrary to our established military policy as presented by an Admiral in charge of COMNAVWESPAC, and as contrary to the intent of Congress as expressed by the China Aid Act of 1948.[28]

Memoranda prepared by James P. Grant, Special Assistant for Rural Reconstruction, and John D. Sumner, Economic Adviser to ECA, also supported the aid to North China policy. Grant particularly stressed the strategic importance of North China as a buffer zone against Russian intrusion, as an industrial area, and as a potential source of raw materials for Japan. Sumner pointed out that Congress knew there was a war in China when it voted for aid, "thereby taking a calculated risk knowing that the aid might be lost." ECA's recommendations were designed to make the risk as minor as possible under the circumstances. It seemed, Sumner added, that if America announced it had given up on North China, the effect would be disastrous on the morale of China's fighting forces.[29]

Backed by the unanimous support of these ECA officials, Ambassador Stuart and Admiral Badger, Roger Lapham traveled to Washington in October to report on the aid mission to the President. Although these men realized that Army and State Department officials did not agree with their plans, they were still puzzled that the military aid appropriated by Congress had not arrived in China. As Stillman's memorandum had indicated, Admiral Badger's recommendations and requests had been approved by the Joint Chiefs of Staff, so there seemed to be no reason for aid to be delayed. There were several explanations proffered. Harlan Cleveland blamed both the American and Chinese governments.

> The U.S. Government agencies involved (the White House, the State Department, and the National Military Establishment) failed in getting the administration of the fund set up quickly, and set up in such a way that decisions on the important questions involved could be rendered promptly. State was made the general coordinating agency; the military services were enabled to take equipment out of stock (against re-payment at replacement cost) at the request of the Chinese. But neither State nor the military department appear to have approached the matter as an operating problem. The result has been delay and confusion about such vital things as prices and delivery arrangements. To this day, for example, the Chinese have not been told definitively that 1945 prices are out.[30]

The Chinese, on the other hand, did not take the initiative which the aid bill legislation had left to them but relied on the United States to take the lead.

Cleveland seems to have been right in assigning deficiencies to both governments. In view of the worsening military situation in China, America moved slowly in implementing military aid. It was not until late in July that funds were made available to participating government agencies for procurement of military equipment. The following month the Army began a survey to determine the availability and the prices of supplies needed by the Chinese. Nationalist government representatives in Washington were also concerned with prices and began investigating commercial sources to try to use the allotted funds for the greatest amount of military equipment obtainable.[31] In September, V. K. Wellington Koo, Chinese Ambassador, presented a revised list of requirements which the Army began to supply. It was not, however, until November 29 that the first shipment arrived in Shanghai.[32] The cause for these delays later became a controversial issue. Marshall's reservations about aid for China were well known and made him and the State Department vulnerable to attacks that they deliberately tried to avert the aid and subvert the wishes of Congress. This accusation became a national issue during the McCarthy era, but was voiced as well in the fall of 1948 in an article by Col. W. Bruce Pirnie which appeared in the *China Monthly*. The Colonel accused the State Department and its agencies of "hamstringing" aid to the Nationalists since the war with Japan, and of restraining American military authorities who were in "vociferous accord" that more should be done for China. If it had not been for the "drag of civil officials in Washington," the Nationalists would have been able to remove the Communist threat from Asia.[33]

Although American leaders in China did not feel a Nationalist victory was possible in the fall of 1948 nor that they could remove the "Communist threat from Asia," they continued to be puzzled over the delays in the shipment of military supplies. On Lapham's trip to report to the President, he inquired many times about the "mystery of the 125 million military aid," but was to receive no satisfactory reply.[34]

He was more successful in his efforts to persuade the administration to allow American naval forces to stay in Tsingtao. There was considerable high level speculation at the time on the threat to Americans in China, particularly in the areas closest to the fighting. During their October 17 meeting, President Truman asked Lapham's opinion on what action the government should take. Lapham noted in his daily record of events that when the President asked about Tsingtao,

> I went overboard plenty. Said I would hate to see the Navy get out of Tsingtao; I felt our Russian friends would be in the next morning, directly or indirectly; and that, after all, possession is nine-tenths of the law.[35]

Lapham felt his argument had been persuasive when the President turned to Admiral Leahy and told him to take up the matter of reinforcement of Tsingtao with the Secretary of Defense.*Two days

---

*Tsingtao also came up in a discussion between Secretary of Defense James Forrestal and White House Naval Aide Robert L. Dennison. Forrestal noted Dennison's remarks in his diary. "He said he felt that if we ever withdrew from China — and by this he referred specifically to the current situation in Tsingtao — we would probably never get back in. I inquired as to the capabilities of carrier aircraft to operate against forces trying to take the port, and he said the roads of ingress to Tsingtao were so concentrated that it would be very easy to operate against any forces which did not have aircraft cover." Walter Millis (ed.), *The Forrestal Diaries* (New York: The Viking Press, 1951), p. 496.

later Lapham called on Admiral Denfeld who agreed that the city should not be abandoned by the Navy, but reported that General Bradley, General Vandenberg and State were "all on the fence and not anxious to run any risk in staying in Tsingtao." Denfeld then showed Lapham a memorandum he had just received from the White House which mentioned Lapham's talk with the President and announced that the decision had been made "to back up Tsingtao." [36] The Navy, then, did not leave their North China base in the fall of 1948, but stayed on until the spring of the following year when Communist advances made evacuation imperative.

In addition to inquiries about military supplies and recommendations on Tsingtao, Lapham's report to the administration included his suggestions for China policy in general. ECA's experience had convinced him that any long-range program should include a thorough re-examination of American objectives in Asia. Did the United States wish to maintain the Open Door, fight communism, support Chiang Kai-shek, or all three? In the meantime, ECA should be granted authority and autonomy in working with provincial governors, independently of the central government, "as long as they retain the degree of local autonomy they now enjoy." * There should be direct American supervision of military expenditures as well. [37]

---

*This suggestion was particularly controversial since it seemed to encourage further fragmentation of China's government. The administration did not wish to assist a possible return of the warlords who had ruled various districts and provinces before Chiang Kai-shek came to power. In a letter to Roy Howard of the Scripps-Howard newspapers, Randall Gould, Editor of the *Shanghai Evening Post & Mercury* noted that the idea of aid to regional leaders had been "distorted to a point where it got too hot to handle and I wonder whether any more will be heard of it. The whole idea has been smeared by 'regional warlord' slime and naturally the ECA people don't want to find themselves involved in any more fights and trouble than they already have on their hands." Gould went on to make some general observations on Sino-American relations. "Now, when you say that from my standpoint the Nanking Government is a little less than perfect, I must admit that you have penetrated right to the middle of my mind. Yet I have never thought its imperfection was wholly original sin. I think our own sentimental attitude and unrealism have fostered every evil from which we now suffer. The question has never been one of finding some instrumentality other than the Kuomintang to combat Communism in China, but of using that instrumentality with sense; and that we have not done. . . . It has been up to us to give some firm guidance and keep some track of how our bounty was used, yet it is only now that we are at the beginning of such treatment and that is mostly due to the realism and ability of people trying to administer an aid program (and I might also include the work of the American Advisory Group) with wholly inadequate weapons provided by the politicians and most of the newspapers at home.

The administration took no immediate action on Lapham's suggestions, other than the decision on Tsingtao. Apparently they continued
to feel, as Butterworth had said earlier, that long-range planning was
impossible with the situation in China so unstable.

Throughout his stay in Washington, however, Lapham continued to
present his policy recommendations to high-ranking officials. In a
meeting with General Albert C. Wedemeyer, he outlined his position in
detail. The General was particularly interested since he had traveled in
China on a presidential mission in 1947. When Lapham finished, "The
General smiled, pulled a copy of his unpublished report out of his
dresser drawer and, pointing to it, said, 'You and I think a great deal
alike.'" [38]

Roger Lapham returned to China on November 4 after three weeks
in Washington. He soon learned that military supplies had not yet
arrived and that both Ambassador Stuart and Admiral Badger were
considerably less optimistic about the situation than they had been
before he left. In a conversation with Allen Griffin, the Admiral "stated
that he considered the military situation utterly hopeless and that he
was convinced that the United States could no longer alter the
situation." [39] A conference with Ambassador Stuart on November 6
revealed he too was discouraged. Although he still felt there was a slim
chance of holding back the Iron Curtain in China, he was less optimistic
than he had been a month earlier. [40]

Meanwhile, the supplies they had hoped might change the course of
the civil war were finally on their way. Negotiations between the Army
suppliers and the Nationalist government representatives resolved the
issue over prices, and arrangements were made for the shipment of
arms to begin. Ports were chosen and free transportation on United
States vessels was provided. The first shipment left the West Coast on
November 9, the second on December 1, and the third on December
16. Only the first shipment, which arrived in Shanghai on November

---

The whole thing is a tragedy which I still think might have been avoided. But some like
[General Joseph W.] Stilwell and [former Ambassador Clarence E.] Gauss who learned
the hard way got pretty bitter and were dismissed as sour-balls, and we have thrown one
enthusiastic amateur after another into this thing. As soon as they lost the amateur sheen
Nanking and Washington vied in getting rid of them. My impression is that certain plain
speech has been kept clear under cover." Letter to Roy W. Howard from Randall Gould,
dated November 6, 1948. Copy in Griffin Papers.

29, was dispersed on the mainland. Communist victories caused the Nationists to order the other two shipments to be diverted to Taiwan.[41]

Part of the military equipment which arrived in Shanghai was left in the city, the other part was sent on to Tsingtao and Tientsin. The Tientsin portion was destined for Fu Tso-yi and in one of history's ironic twists of fate, when the aid so enthusiastically sought for him arrived, it helped cause his Armageddon.

According to historian C. P. Fitzgerald, an agreement had been reached between Communist leader Lin-Piao and the Nationlist General Wei Li-huang who had known one another as cadets in Whampoa Military Academy.* According to the alleged plan, Li Tsung-jen, China's Vice President, would take over the country, declare an armistice and form a coalition government. The army would be integrated and eventually come under Communist control. Fu Tso-yi's armies would retreat into Inner Mongolia, leaving North China free for the Communists to enter. Late in November Fu's troops retreated to Peking and Tientsin as one part of the arrangement. Vice President Li, however, could not obtain enough support to overthrow Chiang, and other problems also delayed enactment of the secret plan. General Fu, meanwhile, had heard of the arrival of American military supplies at Tientsin, and wanted them for his troops and out of the hands of either the Communists or the Nationalist garrison at Tientsin. The delay which resulted when he attempted to get the supplies caused Lin Piao to conclude that Fu would not keep his part of the bargain. Fearing an attack from Fu, therefore, Lin attacked first, capturing the six trainloads of American supplies and causing Fu to retreat into Peking. According to Fitzgerald:

> In all the records of modern warfare no other such improbable operation as the siege of Peking has occurred to enliven the task of the historian. Yet for six weeks, from 13 December 1948, to 22 January 1949, this strange siege continued . . .
> The Communists did not press the siege, because they had no intention

*Rumors of a secret agreement between the Communists and members of Chiang's government were widespread. John Melby recorded his skeptical analysis in his diary on July 13, 1948. "Suddenly there is a rash of reports that Chou En-lai is secretly in Peiping dickering with Fu Tso-yi, who commands in North China, and with Li Tsung-jen. It is difficult to believe this is true. It is no longer possible to judge any sources of information with any reliability." John F. Melby, *The Mandate of Heaven: Record of a Civil War, China 1945-49* (Toronto, Canada: University of Toronto Press, 1968), p. 283.

of either damaging an historic city which they intended to restore to its ancient place as the capital or of getting a bad name by injuring the inhabitants. No possibility of relief existed. The nearest Kuomintang forces, except the besieged defenders of Tientsin, were more than five hundred miles away in the Yang Tze Valley, and still retreating. The siege of Peking must end in one way; it was only a question of time and of 'face.'[42]

Lin Piao and Fu Tso-yi, each offended by what he suspected was treachery on the part of the other, could not negotiate a settlement. Finally, Lin was replaced by another commander and Fu surrendered.[43] The part that American aid played in the siege of Peking and in the career of General Fu Tso-yi was hardly the role American officials had envisioned.*

DISPERSAL OF RESIDUAL SUPPLIES

Communist victories in the fall of 1948 caused ECA officials to focus their attention on a new aspect of the aid program — how to handle American supplies in areas being lost by the Nationalists. This question of dispersal of supplies became the second major difference of opinion between Washington and ECA. The administration wished to keep aid goods from helping the Communists. ECA leaders, who wished to stay in contact with any *de facto* government — Nationalist, Communist, or coalition — thought commodities should continue to be dispersed as a means of keeping a line of communication open.

In November, Allen Griffin wrote a lengthy memorandum to Harlan Cleveland. He said that in China they were becoming aware through "news accounts, the attitude of Embassy officials and quotations from Washington that indicate that United States policy towards China may be fixing itself in the position that no aid would or should be extended" to either a coalition government or a Communist government. Griffin could not figure out how this attitude could serve American goals:

> Over here one may reasonably ask the question, what purpose does this apparently hardening attitude serve . . . Certainly this attitude does not bolster Nationalist morale because there actually is no Nationalist

*In the autumn of 1949, General Fu Tso-yi was appointed the Minister of Water Conservancy in the Communist government. Stuart Schram, *Mao Tse-tung* (Baltimore, Maryland: Penguin Books, 1966), p. 243n.

morale. Certainly, also, it extends the unreasonable hopes and wishful thinking of a handful of people in high places, to the effect that United States aid will pour from a gigantic cornucopia to save them from something from which they are incapable of saving themselves in even the smallest measure. This attitude also does not win approval from American and foreign interests in China because they can see nothing constructive in an attitude that is actually antagonistic to their interests in this country. Moreover, it obviously is not discouraging the Communists from continuing their sweep across the face of China. Certainly they won't fight less well because we threaten to do no business with them. Therefore, perhaps one may assume that this attitude on the one hand is released and kept in the news for public consumption at home in the supposition that there is some good in doing that sort of thing; or, second, it is a policy that the United States government is definitely moving towards.

Let me tell you what I think it indicates. That is that the United States of America, this time, is preparing to draw the Iron Curtain around China by its own volition because of its own policy. Now that is an extraordinary thing for us to do when our entire program has been based on holding the Iron Curtain back. As a matter of fact, you have heard Roger Lapham repeatedly say that ECA is here to hold back the Iron Curtain . . . .

I have no illusions about the Communist leaders. I do not believe that there is any way that we can reform them or alter them or make them anything less than Marxist Communist leaders. I do not belong to that rather large school of Old China Hands who believe it can be "different in China" in that respect. However, I most emphatically believe that the United States of America has a fighting chance to separate the Communism of China from control by Moscow. . . .

How will we do it? We will prepare to negotiate with whatever Chinese Government controls China . . . and not slam the door. If that Government chooses to slam the door, then that will be that. But our position will have been consistent in the eyes of the world and in the eyes of multitudes of the intelligent people in China who would thereafter bear no grudge against our country for having failed them. Certainly a condition of aid would be the continuing operation in China of United States and other foreign business . . . as private enterprise . . . This would include freedom of travel of foreigners in China on business or for pleasure without hindrance. It would include freedom of association with Chinese of any and all classes as well as freedom of travel of Chinese outside of their own country and the maintenance of exchange students, etc. It would include the unhampered operations of USIS libraries and news distribution in any part of China. In short, it would provide for all the things that the Russian Iron Curtain has been pulled down to prevent. Utilizing that freedom within China we then could apply our intelligence and our efforts and our patience not to stir up another revolution but to develop in every way we can a cleavage between Soviet Russia and China, a greater dependence by China upon the western nations. In short, we will act to prevent, rather than to help, the surrounding of this country by an iron curtain, and will not liquidate the interests of the USA in this important part of the world. To me that is a cold-blooded realism, and it is a whale of a fight.[44]

Roger Lapham agreed with Griffin's analysis of the situation, and on November 26, 1948 he addressed a cable to Paul Hoffman outlining four alternatives. One, complete the present program as long as "ECA personnel had freedom of action, cooperation from local authorities on distribution arrangements and permission to tell the Chinese people the source of the goods." Two, continue the same program "only to the extent of allowing distribution of foodstuffs and other commodities already landed or en route to China." Three, stop or re-route all shipments and disperse only goods on hand. Four, stop or re-route all shipments and try to reclaim goods in China. Lapham stated that he recommended one or two and strongly opposed three or four.[45] He felt the United States should try to maintain contacts with whatever government took over in China. Paul Hoffman supported Lapham's ideas and tried to obtain a decision on the matter before he left Washington for an extensive trip which was to include four days in China.

In a memorandum to President Truman, Hoffman recommended alternative number one from Lapham's cable. This action, he felt, would give America a propaganda advantage over the Communists since it would belie the Communist claim that the United States had imperialistic intentions in China, and if they refused the aid materials, the onus would be on them and the psychological advantage would be America's.[46] Hoffman also tried to persuade the Congressional Watchdog Committee, and found them to be generally in favor of Lapham's suggestion. They were sensitive to Communist claims of American imperialism and wanted to avoid inadvertently giving credence to these claims.[47] Hoffman was less encouraged by his meeting with Under Secretary of State Robert Lovett who seemed indefinite about what action should be taken and in Hoffman's estimation was "more concerned about what was feasible in the eyes of Congress and the American public."[48]

Lovett's attitude may have reflected the administration's equivocation on the China situation. At a National Security Council meeting on

November 3, Secretary of Defense James Forrestal recorded in his diary, there had been an "inconclusive discussion of whether the shipments of supplies and equipment to the Chinese Nationalist government could be delayed and whether the distribution of supplies and equipment in China could" [49] be regulated. At a Cabinet meeting on November 22, the Secretary found out the situation in China was rapidly deteriorating. Recently, more than thirty of the "Nationalist government divisions surrendered, with equipment, and these included a number of American-trained divisions. . . . The net result is the loss of a vast amount of American-bought equipment to the Communists." [50] Four days later at another Cabinet meeting, Forrestal learned that the military deterioration of the Nationalists had accelerated. "Equipment for 33 divisions, including 297,000 rifles, a large amount of automatic weapons, 105 and 155 millimeter guns and antiaircraft weapons, have been captured by Soviets.*" [51]

Under the circumstances, Hoffman's suggestion may have seemed untimely and no decision was made before he departed on December 5. His trip had been undertaken on the urgings of Roger Lapham who felt that Hoffman needed a first hand view of the situation, and that his presence in China would demonstrate that the United States was not yet abandoning its aid program. When he arrived in Shanghai, Hoffman received a memorandum from Lapham in which the mission leader outlined his views on conditions in the country, and presented his recommendations for China policy. Lapham pointed out the military deterioration, the inefficiency of the Nationalists, the desperate economic problems, and the poor leadership of Chiang Kai-shek. Lapham did not mince words in his assessment, and blamed many of the problems ECA had had on the:

> Inefficiency and incompetence of the Nanking Government — even after making due allowance for the handicaps imposed on any government fighting a civil war. The Chinese Communists are no dumbbells. They have lost no opportunities in emphasizing that the United States is spending its funds to assist a government dominated by an obstinate and narrow-minded man whose prestige among his own people is slipping rapidly because of constant military as well as economic reverses. We are today witnessing a Shakespearean tragedy — the head of a government pulling down the roof and walls of his own house.[52]

*Please note that Forrestal referred to the Chinese Communists as the "Soviets."

The aid program was difficult to administer under the circumstances, according to Lapham, and was further plagued by Communist propaganda which blamed China's problems on American aid and American policy. He recommended short and long-range goals for the United States. Under short-term goals, he reiterated his suggestions in his November 26 cable and emphasized that abandonment of the aid program would cause greater suffering for the Chinese. As for long-term goals, the most important continued to be the need for a decision on overall objectives for China policy. As an adjunct to this, the government should reach some conclusion as to the nature of the Chinese Communists. Were they led by Moscow, were they part of the Politburo, or were they Chinese patriots only using the Communist name? Lapham's urgings for policy decisions reflected the uneasiness he had felt thoughout his stay. American goals seemed vague and indeterminate and the aid mission not only suffered from the lack of guidance from the State Department but also from a noticeable lack of coordination with other American agencies in the field.[53] It seemed to this successful businessman and efficient administrator an inept way to handle policy matters, and a source of constant frustration for men who had to cope with the day to day problems of running the aid program.

During Hoffman's four day stay in China, he participated in dawn to dusk briefings and conferences on the economic and military situation. He met with high-ranking American and Chinese government officials and with a number of other groups as well. On December 12 he spoke with representatives of the Volunteer Agencies who requested a grant of $20,000,000 from the United States. The same day he met with CUSA representatives who "suggested reallocation of present ECA unexpended funds, as well as aid for second quarter 1949 and fiscal year 1949-50." At a breakfast meeting the following morning, he was joined by James Grant, ECA representative in Tientsin, and Cheng Tao-ju, a civilian assistant of Fu Tso-yi, who discussed the situation in North China. Later he met with twenty scientists and civic leaders of Shanghai who presented their views. On December 14 he was brought up-to-date on JCRR activities by Chiang Mon-lin and Raymond Moyer. He then flew to Nanking where he met with Foreign Minister Wang Shih-chieh, and later, at a conference in Ambassador Stuart's home, he discussed Lapham's November 26 cable with members of ECA and

American military leaders. This was followed by a short meeting with Chiang Kai-shek and dinner that evening at the President's home. Lapham's calendar of events noted, "Dinner party of 24 at President's house, with pictures taken before dinner. Americans present included Ambassador, Clark, Merchant, Admiral Badger, General Barr, Lapham, Griffin, Sumner and Crow *"⁵⁴ The following day Hoffman returned to Shanghai and took off from there for Korea.

During his brief stay in China, Hoffman's views on the dispersal of American aid were brought into the open at a Shanghai Press Conference. The meeting with the press was held on December 13 at the American Club with Hoffman, Ambassador Stuart, Roger Lapham, and Allen Griffin at the speaker's table. The questions centered on what actions would be taken by the American government in relation to the aid program if another government took over in China. The first reporter asked, "Would you say there is any chance that the purely relief work of ECA would be continued under a Communist regime here, or a coalition regime?" Hoffman answered, "If it was a coalition government which, in our opinion, represented all the people, I would certainly recommend that relief be continued." He went on to point out that his recommendation would not necessarily be accepted and that he was sure that, "If it was a coalition obviously and completely Communist, I would say the chances are that our Government would not favor the continuation of such support." In the period when the United States was not sure which kind of government prevailed in the country, however, Hoffman explained he would "certainly recommend the continuation of our aid under the same conditions that now prevail." ECA at the present time had "no thought of diverting any ships . . . that are carrying either food or raw materials."⁵⁵

The views Hoffman articulated at the press conference supported the recommendation made by Roger Lapham in his November 26 cable. There were certain stipulations the new governing agencies in China would have to meet according to a memorandum Hoffman took back to Washington with him. If they met the conditions, however, aid would continue to be distributed to them. The requirements ECA had

*Ambassador Stuart; Lewis Clark, Counselor to the Ambassador; Livingston Merchant, Counselor to the Ambassador; Admiral Oscar Badger; General David Barr, Head of the Military Advisory Group; Lapham; Griffin; John D. Sumner, ECA Economic Adviser; Philip K. Crowe, Special ECA Representative in Nanking.

in mind would be defined in an agreement with the new governing body after a Nationalist defeat.

> The local *de facto* authority must:
> 1. Allow ECA to distribute supplies for the benefit of the people with the help of local agencies.
> 2. Allow ECA American and non-American personnel ... freedom from search or seizure with respect to themselves, their personal effects, vehicles, and living and office space, and equipment used by them or by ECA.
> 3. Allow American and non-American staff of ECA ... freedom of inspection of commodities so supplied to determine whether stocks of such commodities are in fact being properly stored, used, and distributed for the purposes.
> 4. Allow American and non-American staff of ECA to be free to move about and communicate where supplies are distributed, with other ECA posts in China and with points outside of China.
> 5. Provide local currency.
> 6. Allow ECA personnel to make announcements, statements in newspapers, etc.[56]

This agreement for the continued dispersal of aid met with Hoffman's approval.[57] Lapham's other suggestions also met with favor in ECA's Washington office. Harlan Cleveland wrote the head of the China mission complimenting his policy suggestions. Lapham's reply expressed his appreciation of Cleveland's approval and went on to say:

> Personally, I think the Far Eastern Division of the State Department needs plenty prodding. I have had the feeling right along that some people in that division, as well as in the Embassy here, resented ECA intrusion in the foreign policy field and have been reluctant to keep the Chief of the Mission as fully advised on policy and military developments as he was entitled to be. I am sure that is not a deliberate omission on the part of the Ambassador, and I am frank to say that I don't think the Ambassador has been told everything by his own staff.[58]

Lapham was probably even unhappier with the State Department when he discovered that his suggestions, which Hoffman had articulated in the Shanghai Press Conference, were met in Washington without approbation. The first indications that there might be a controversy over what Hoffman had said were revealed to him on a stop-over in Hawaii on his return trip. He was informed that quotes from his press conference indicated he was in favor of continued aid to

China even if a Communist dominated coalition took over. Hoffman replied that that was not the exact meaning of his remarks. "We would probably continue feeding people until the State Department decided whether the new government were qualified for such aid." ECA, he said, "feeds people, not governments.*"[59]

Three days later Hoffman met with President Truman. After the meeting, his comments to the press were "guarded," and he announced that funds would be frozen for the industrial reconstruction and replacement part of the aid program.[60] Earlier the same day there was another indication that ECA was a bit out of favor with the administration. A White House press officer had announced that the agency had been asked to clear all appointments of policy-making personnel with the Executive since at present very few of ECA's people were "known over here." [61] The move implied that the motives of those who favored continued aid to coalition governments might be viewed with suspicion.

Early in January, 1949, Harlan Cleveland informed Lapham that Hoffman's opinions, expressed at the Shanghai Press Conference, were "now called into serious question, and it may be that you will get before long a cable indicating that no supplies will be given to any area or group run by a government that includes Communists." [62] The subject had come up "at a couple of National Security Council meetings and at least one Cabinet meeting," and there was a general consensus that the supplies which were already in China should be distributed under the supervision of the *de facto* authorities. The State Department would not go beyond that and was "taking quite firmly the line that the

---

*Mr. Hoffman's remarks at his December 13, 1948, press conference in Shanghai were unusual enough to evoke an interesting response from a Communist publication in Hong Kong. An article entitled "An Open Letter to Mr. Paul G. Hoffman" appeared on December 18, 1948. The article praised Hoffman for bringing up the possibility of continued aid to a new government. "If your outlook as such could be underwritten by the White House and Congress, the U.S. policy in China would indeed take on a complexion quite different from what it appears now." China, the article went on to say, would welcome foreign aid "be it part of Marshall Plan or of Molotov Plan," because "there will be no such thing as a closed-door policy on our part." The article noted, however, that aid would not be accepted if it had any political strings. "After emerging from the present Revolution, the Chinese will be ever more vigilant over foreign imperialists' designs and will have grown of age to distinguish poison from medicine no matter how sugar-coated is the poison and with whatever velvet gloves it is handled." *Far Eastern Bulletin*, December 18, 1948. Reprint of article in Griffin Papers.

Chinese Communists should be left to stew in their own juices, with no help whatever from the U.S. for the people in the areas controlled by them." [63] At a meeting in Robert Lovett's office, Paul Hoffman presented his views which he said "were those of about 95% of the people he talked to in China." After Hoffman made his statement, there was a lengthy discussion wherein:

> It became clear that Mr. Hoffman and Mr. Lovett disagreed fundamentally on the basic approach to the problem — Mr. Hoffman speaking in favor of continuing to stay in China and trying to prevent Russian domination in China by demonstrating the continued friendship of America for the Chinese people, while Mr. Lovett generally believed such an approach to be unwise, reverting several times to the theme that such a policy was not in accordance with the China Aid Act or what he believed to be the consensus of opinion in Congress. . . .
> Toward the end of the meeting, Mr. Hoffman summarized the disagreement between the two agencies in the following terms: "You want to walk out of China," he said to Mr. Lovett, "but if we are going out of China, I want to be thrown out." [64]

The opposite views of the two men were again brought out when they appeared at a Cabinet meeting. Hoffman said America should continue to give aid to the Chinese under a regional plan if for no other reason than that it was the best way to refute the propaganda claims of the Communists. Lovett said the action recommended by Hoffman would have a detrimental effect on American efforts in other parts of the world and would be an obvious exception to an otherwise consistent global policy of anti-communism. A poll of the Cabinet revealed they opposed Hoffman's position on the matter, with the exception of stocks already in Tsingtao which were to go to Tientsin when conditions permitted.

On January 15 President Truman made his decision, which was imparted to the China Mission by Harlan Cleveland:

> Following policy ruling has been made by President after full discussion all issues involved:
> A. That this Government would continue to support through the implementation of the China Aid Act the present Chinese Government or legal successor Government which pursues an Anti-Communist policy. However should a Government come into power which comes to terms with the Chinese Communists all aid should cease irrespective of whether the Communists are in numerical ascendancy or not. The Preceding sentence means of course that aid should cease to those areas that

come under the control of a Government in which the Communists participate.

B. When the Chinese Communists either directly or indirectly through a coalition Government take control over any area all ECA supplies ashore or in the process of being unloaded can be distributed under conditions similar to those now prevailing. However ECA supplies which have not reached such ports should be diverted elsewhere.

Cleveland's cable concluded with the notice that the State Department was advising the Embassy of the decision, and with the caution that "extreme care should be taken maintain secrecy this policy which could have widespread repercussions if divulged." [65]

Allen Griffin, who was in Washington for meetings in January, 1949, further informed Roger Lapham that:

Various conferences with various people, plus decisions that have been made at the highest levels, indicate without any question of a doubt that policy you would consider quite negative has now become fixed. It is probable that this policy will remain in that frozen condition for quite some months to come. That is the indication that was given to me when I asked the specific question. Paul Hoffman put up a real battle in favor of the policy that you and your senior staff advocated. I consider that under the circumstances prevailing here, he carried it on in a manner that was daring as well as courageous. [66]

The policy which ECA officials deplored represented the growing rigidity of America's anti-communist stance in the Cold War and revealed a complete turnabout from the attempts for a coalition government in 1946. As Ambassador Stuart recalled, "In course of time I received the most explicit instructions not to encourage or in any way assist in the formation of a coalition which included Communists. American official policy had seemingly therefore completely reversed itself." [67]

Communist victories in the fall and the takeover of northern cities in January contributed to this change in policy. American officials had also become more apprehensive about the true nature of China's Communists. The cherished notion that they were merely "agrarian reformers" or might follow a "Titoistic" independence from Moscow were not born out by recent pronouncements of Communist leaders. For example, an article by Mao Tse-tung in November, 1948, stated that:

The particular task of the Chinese Communists is to unite all revolutionary forces within the whole country to drive out the aggressive forces of

American imperialism, overthrow the reactionary rule of the Kuomintang and establish a . . . Democratic People's Republic.[68]

Liu Shao-chi in a December 14, 1948, article wrote:

> At present the world is divided into two mutually antagonistic camps; on the one hand is American imperialism and its stooges in the various countries of the world — the reactionaries of the various countries. This is the world imperialist camp. On the other hand is the Soviet Union and the new democratic countries of Eastern Europe, the national liberation movements of Greece, and the people's democratic forces of all countries in the world. This is the world anti-imperialist camp. At a time when these two camps are in a tense conflict with each other, peoples must stand either on the one side or on the other . . . Neutrality — standing neither on the one side nor on the other — is impossible. The oppressed nations of the world, the proletariat and the people's democratic forces of all the countries must all unite together with the Soviet Union, must unite with the new democratic countries of Eastern Europe in order to defeat the American imperialist plan for world enslavement.[69]

The inflammatory words from China's Communist leaders and their military victories seemed, in the eyes of American policy makers, to fit into a threatening pattern with the Russian blockade of Berlin which was in its seventh month. The desire to prevent American supplies from helping Communists anywhere seemed reasonable.

The policy change, however, caused some problems for the ECA mission in Tientsin. In December, the Tientsin office had received instructions to remain open and to "carry on — even under a Communist take-over — normal food rationing and commodity distribution activities." These instructions, according to James T. Ivy, Head of ECA's Tientsin Office, seemed to support Hoffman's announcement that "ECA's purpose was to help 'the people', and that ECA's activities would be continued even under a Communist-dominated regime, provided it respected certain 'personal freedoms'." Under the December instructions, the Tientsin office continued with the previous ECA program for the city. One month later the instructions reflected the abrupt change of policy. ECA's Tientsin office notified that they were "under no circumstances to contact Communist authorities, or have anything to do with them." This directive was a "repudiation of the 'Marching Orders' under which we had been working; and it left us sitting in Tientsin, absolutely empty-handed." To Ivy it seemed unfortunate that the new instructions left them with:

No potential arguments whatever to use in dealing with the Communists;
no "potential" supplies which we might have been able to use as bait for
some sort of special dispensation and unofficial arrangement with them.
Our flour stocks, insufficient for even one 10 day period, were not much
of a bargaining weapon; and the fact that we could offer them the hope
of no further shipments deprived us of any weapons we otherwise might
have had. Therefore, we could only sit and await confiscation of our
stocks, against which we could do nothing but protest forcefully though
futilely; and to dispose of our equipment and supplies (after we received
the closure order) as best we could.[70]

Although Ivy disagreed with the quick change of orders which left him
devoid of bargaining possibilities during the takeover of Tientsin, in
his overall assessment of future relations with the Communists he felt
certain the new government would not accept American "Economic
Cooperation."

To do so would be to go against the main theme of their intensely
nationalistic propaganda, and would cause them to lose face; and it *may be*
(we certainly have no evidence to support this) that "orders from Moscow" forbid the Chinese Communists' acceptance of U.S. aid or
cooperation.[71]

Before the new government totally rejected help from the United
States, however, Roger Lapham still hoped to keep America's "foot in
the door" with some sort of aid and with what he considered a "positive" approach to China policy.

FUTURE AMERICAN POLICY

Taiwan* — Throughout most of its history the island of Taiwan had
been a Chinese possession. In 1895 it was ceded to Japan and remained
under Japanese rule until the end of the war in 1945, when it was again
restored to China. Except for minor commercial exchanges, American
interest in the island had been minimal; no cultural, philanthropic, or
missionary groups were in operation before World War II. During and
after the war, however, Taiwan began to figure in American plans and
became a factor in overall China policy.

In July, 1948, ECA opened a regional office in the capital city,
Taipei, and ECA's Regional Director, Loris P. Craig, made an extensive "pre-project survey." Throughout the mission many American

---

*Taiwan is also known as Formosa which means "beautiful" in Portuguese.

supplies were diverted to the island when the Communists threatened mainland dispersal centers.[72]

Early in 1949, American interest sharply increased, and policy makers began to re-evaluate the island's strategic and economic potential. In February, Henry J. Tarring, Jr. of the J. G. White Engineering Corporation was sent to begin work on an industrial reconstruction program.[73] Shortly thereafter, JCRR's program was expanded as well.

Roger Lapham was concerned about Taiwan policy and in a memorandum to the Secretary of State and the Embassy in Nanking he outlined his ideas. His recommendations, he pointed out, were based on three days he had spent looking over the situation on the island, on discussions he had had with Admirals Ramsey and Badger at Tsingtao, with Ambassador Stuart, with "responsible mainland Chinese who were not close followers of Chiang Kai-shek," and with General Douglas MacArthur in Tokyo on January 30. MacArthur expressed what was to become a popular point of view in the United States in the years to come, a view that was later known as the "domino theory." According to the General, the Communists should be kept out of Taiwan because if they were allowed to take over, "it would necessitate withdrawal of the United States forces from Japan, Okinawa, Guam and the whole chain of islands from the North to Australia." America's line of defense, if this happened, would be on the mainland of North and South America. He not only opposed a Communist takeover of the island, but hoped the Kuomintang could be kept out as well. To Lapham, he said,

> The pussy-footing of the United States Government in refusing to accept the responsibility for conditions in China should be cast overboard and you should be permitted to take whatever measures are necessary in order to carry out your program even to the extent of direct supervision of the economic control of Formosa in order to prevent the exploitation of the Island by the Kuomintang party organization and to insure that the Communists are prevented from extending their domination.

In the interview, MacArthur was also very critical of what he called General George Marshall's "blind spot in respect to the Far East," which had enabled the Communists "to close us out and advance their frontier to the southern limits of Asia. This is a strategical blunder which our children will be paying for for a hundred years."

> It is even worse than the blunder by which Berlin and Vienna were cut off from any land connections in the control of Britain and the United

States. Any second lieutenant could have appreciated the seriousness of these blunders. It is explainable only by the utter simplicity and the obviousness of the issues. Truman, Eisenhower, and Marshall must have been utterly tired and worn out by their efforts during the war to permit Berlin and Vienna to be cut off from any corridor of approach from our side.[74]

As a result of his talk with MacArthur and other officials, Lapham made several suggestions to the State Department on American policy for Taiwan. First, the island should not be allowed to fall into the hands of the Communists. Second, the government should not serve the interest of Chiang Kai-shek, but the interests of the people of the island. Third, any effort made by the United States should not be half-hearted like the program for mainland China, but a forthright and emphatic program.[75] In a press release from Taipei, on February 9, Lapham said he would ask for more aid for Taiwan on his forthcoming trip to Washington,[76] but two days later he was cautioned by Hoffman not to mention the island in his public statements until after they had had a "chance to go over the whole problem here when you arrive."[77] Hoffman was probably somewhat apprehensive that ECA would get into another policy controversy with the State Department. Lapham heeded his admonition, but increased American interest in Taiwan had not escaped the attention of *New York Times'* reporter, Henry Lieberman, who on February 18, 1949, wrote that the United States was interested in the island as an ECA aid outlet. He said ECA was exploring the situation and cited as evidence Lapham's recent trip, the coming trip of the rural reconstruction commission, and surveys that Westinghouse engineers were making of the island's electrical power potential.[78]

The reporter would have been even more assured of American interests had he known of the State Department trip of Livingston Merchant, who traveled to Taiwan on February 26 on what Allen Griffin in a letter to Lapham, called a "delicate mission." So delicate, in fact, that he cautioned Lapham "not to refer to Merchant's visit to Formosa other than to say that you hear that he has taken a trip there."[79]

Urgings for Lapham's discretion from Hoffman and Griffin applied to public pronouncements. In private, he continued to push his policy recommendations. A memorandum to Hoffman outlined his views on the subject of Taiwan. A program supporting the native population of the island should be the number one goal of American policy. With this in mind, a Chinese governor other than Chiang Kai-shek should be appointed at once and should have an American with an American staff to help and advise him. Lapham further suggested that industrial replacement and reconstruction, rural reconstruction and medical programs should be instituted under American personnel. In his opinion the United States should secure the island first and then, when "we have placed our people in position and get the situation under control, I believe we should then clarify our intentions by making the U. N. take over the trusteeship."[80]

Lapham reiterated his suggestions in a March 9 memorandum to Paul Hoffman. He emphasized, "We should use our influence to prevent further exploitation of the island by the mainland people — the number of Nationalist refugees now pouring into that island should be restricted." He did not want Taiwan to be become a Nationalist stronghold and advised that "above all we should prevent the island becoming a Chinese military base to operate against the Communists on the mainland."[81]

Meanwhile, Henry Tarring's survey group had come up with an estimate of industrial reconstruction for Taiwan. Allen Griffin commented on the aid proposal in a letter to Roger Lapham. "As you know by now, Tarring and his engineers have turned in a grand total ECA cost (i.e., recommendation) of $21,388,000, which is an increase of more than $7,000,000 over the original tentative allocation for projects." Griffin agreed with Lapham, however, that additional aid should not go to Taiwan unless the United States had almost complete control.

> I consider that it would be extremely unfortunate if this program were committed without making sure of American economic guidance of *all* the affairs of that island plus the political safety of the island. If this place can't be put in the bag for sure, we'd better stay out rather than invite mainland antagonism to the attempt to do a big thing and its failure.[82]

On May 11, Griffin again expressed his opinion in a memorandum to Harlan Cleveland. He said his view on the industrial reconstruction program was "entirely negative." More and more Chinese officials were leaving the mainland and the island would soon be "the last retreat of the Right Wing of the Kuomintang Party." Since they were an extremely wealthy group of people, Griffin felt they could easily finance any reconstruction projects needed on Taiwan.* [83]

His opinions were reinforced after a four day trip to the island, and on June 1, he informed the Secretary of State that he was "most strongly against" the allocation of $17,000,000 for an industrial program. If the United States were not willing to secure the island, additional aid appropriations would be wasted. [84]

The Truman administration apparently agreed with Griffin and decided to delay further reconstruction aid. The firm measures Lapham and Griffin recommended to keep the island out of the hands of either the Nationalists or the Communists, however, represented a commitment administration leaders were not yet prepared to make. On March 1, Harlan Cleveland reported the results of a National Security Council meeting to Paul Hoffman. When American policy toward Taiwan came up, a report from the Joint Chiefs of Staff revealed that although they felt the island was important from a strategic point of view, they opposed military intervention "in the event that the political and economic steps already approved by the National Security Council do not succeed." A State Department paper, at the same meeting, outlined the "steps to be taken in getting the political and economic program underway." One paragraph of the paper, Cleveland reported, continued "to reflect the State Department assumption that a 'vigorous economic program' can be conducted behind a screen of anonymity." [85] Apparently the State Department continued to hope it could keep America's interest in the island from being further grist for the Communist propaganda mill. Although Lapham got the impression at a meeting with the Secretary of State that the department wanted to do something for the people of Taiwan and wished to keep either the Nationalists or the Communists from taking over, the United States government was definitely not prepared to take strong or decisive measures. Lapham's suggestion not to go ahead on Taiwan "without assurance of military protection if necessary had been turned down at the highest levels." The decision, at the moment, "was that ECA should drag its feet in procurements of any capital expendi-

* Thomas E. Dewey talked with Henry Tarring in 1951 and found out that, "Without a dollar of American aid for the first year and three quarters, the whole Formosa industrial plant was restored by Chinese efforts under Mr. Tarring's guidance." Thomas E. Dewey, *Journey to the Far Pacific*, p. 309.

ture although meanwhile we could go ahead with JCRR and a fertilizer program." [86] A more precise policy would not be forthcoming, Lapham was sure, "even though every day we wait means the Kuomintang boys are strengthening their hold in the island." * [87]

Lapham was to continue to be concerned with the fate of Taiwan. In the memorandum he and Griffin prepared for Ambassador-at-Large Philip Jessup in the fall of 1949, they described conditions and recommended American action.

> The deteriorated condition of this island is well known to our authorities. Administration by Kuomintang reactionary elements continues; hundreds of thousands of military personnel are quartered on the island in various stages of training and various conditions of morale; most of the military stores that remain in the possession of the Nationalist Government are located on the island; and Taiwan is being used as a base for the so-called blockade of the Communist held Mainland and for the harassment of centers of population. The provincial administration and the conduct of the military operations on that island are continued testimony to the inefficiency, the corruption, and the persistent ignorance of the Kuomintang leadership. The chief jeopardy to this area comes from within rather than from the dangers of invasion at the present time. It is the opinion of the writers of this memorandum that the United States should undertake energetically, with or without the assistance of other powers, to seek to make Taiwan the Switzerland of the Pacific. The strongest and most skillful means should be employed in an effort to bring about a government of the island that is friendly to the United States and to the aspiration of the resident population there. The use of Taiwan as a base for military operation against the mainland should be stopped. Necessary reforms should be compelled. The United States Fleet should then guarantee the security of the island against invasion. The population in the Far East outside of Japan. The people there would

---

* After the mission had virtually come to an end on the mainland, ECA leaders were still unsure of the administration's plans for Taiwan. On June 23, 1949, Harlan Cleveland wrote Paul Hoffman that he felt ECA should. "request a State Department policy decision on future operations on Taiwan. There are three possibilities: (a) a full scale economic program for which ample funds are now available; (b) a continuation of the present scale of operations to February 15, 1950 (this might cost $5-10 million with the principal item being fertilizer; the J.G. White contract for technical assistance might also be continued); and (c) a tapering off of the present program quite soon. Unless it is decided to proceed with (a), the deterioration of conditions on Taiwan makes a fairly rapid tapering off seem the more attractive of the other possibilities." Memorandum to Paul Hoffman from Harlan Cleveland, June 23, 1949. Griffin Papers.

welcome the type of intervention which was conducted to preserve their liberty, and the autonomy of the island. If this can be brought to pass without the institution of American military bases in Taiwan, so much the better. However, it is firmly believed that unless the most forceful action is taken to bring about the conditions recommended here, it will be impossible to preserve this island under a government friendly to the United States.[88]

When these strong steps were not undertaken and the Nationalists were definitely in charge, Lapham was more reluctant to recommend firm and unilateral American action. In a letter to H. Medill Sarkisian in January, 1950, he said he still believed that if the military leaders felt the island was essential to the United States a move should be made to get rid of Chiang Kai-shek and set up a protectorate. However, he just could not "stomach the thought of using our Navy to protect Chiang in Formosa." [89] A few months later Lapham's views which represented the middle ground in the growing controversy over Taiwan, were to meet with partial approval in American policy. At the start of the Korean War in June, 1950, the Seventh Fleet moved to protect Taiwan and the American policy of massive help for the island, both economic and military, began.* This was in line with what the ECA leader had advocated. What he had hoped to avoid, however, was also implicit in the new policy — the United States was protecting Chiang Kai-shek and the Nationalists' hegemony.

THE QUESTION OF ADDITIONAL AID FOR CHINA

The resolution of Taiwan policy was more than a year in the future in the spring of 1949 when Lapham made his recommendations to the government on the subject. He was also concerned on his trip to Washington with another aspect of policy, continued aid. The ECA program he had sent to China to carry out was to expire in April and he hoped to convince the leaders in the capital to continue the program.

The Truman administration's position in the preceding year had become increasingly opposed to further bolstering of Chiang Kai-shek. Although more strongly anti-communist than before, the United States judged that the Nationalists were not successfully opposing the

*By mid-1971, The United States had spent $5,425,000,000 on economic and military aid to Taiwan, second only to Vietnam and Korea in the Far East. *U.S. News & World Report,* November 15, 1971, p. 21.

"enemy" and instead were wasting American resources. American officials were not, therefore, amenable to Chiang Kai-shek's requests for additional aid in November, 1948.[90]

The Generalissimo asked President Truman for additional aid on November 18, but received no firm commitment.[91] Later the same month, Madame Chiang planned a trip to the United States in the hope she could be more persuasive than her husband.* She notified American officials of her trip and requested transportation on a Navy plane. At a Cabinet meeting Marshall brought up the subject of the trip and asked if she should be allowed to come. According to Forrestal who was present at the meeting, "The President said yes."[92] When Lapham heard of the trip, he wrote Hoffman of his disapproval. He felt the use of an American military plane for her transportation would lead to the false impression that the United States continued to give whole-hearted support to the Nationalists, and would especially mislead the non-Communist Chinese who were hoping the Generalissimo would step aside. Lapham felt the only good that could come from the trip would be "if Madame were received coolly in the United States and convince her that the Gimo should retire."[93] Madame Chiang's exhortations for aid were not met with approval on her trip and, although this was not the only reason, it strongly contributed to what Lapham hoped for — Chiang Kai-shek retired in January, 1949.** The issue of aid for China, however, did not retire with him.

---

* Madame Chiang's charm and persuasive powers had been successful in previous visits to the United States, especially during World War II. She was well-known and popular, and a poll taken late in December, 1948, placed her second only to Eleanor Roosevelt in a list of the world's most admired women. "Public Opinion Polls in China," *Far Eastern Survey*, XIX (July 12, 1950), 131. Her personal request for more aid was accompanied by a number of messages to American officials from many groups in China. For example, on December 1, 1948, sixteen women's organizations sent a joint telegram to President Truman, Secretary Marshall, and Eleanor Roosevelt asking them to support additional aid. The President and Secretary of State received an appeal from the Chinese National Federation of Labor Unions, representing 5,000,000 workers. A message from "Shanghai leading businessmen, industrialists, bankers, labor organizers, doctors, lawyers, accountants, and newspaper men" asked for more help. They promised there would be political reform in the government and pledged to "fight the Communists to the finish." One thousand school teachers from Nanking asked for more aid, pointed out that China was as important as Europe, that the Communists were definitely not "agrarian reformers," and that "administrative deficiency in China cannot be held as a reason for not giving aid to us. Experiences have told us that no thorough political reform can be carried out without first defeating the Communists." The United Nations

Nationalist representatives continued to request military and economic aid for their government. Chinese Ambassador V.K. Wellington Koo called on Secretary of State Dean Acheson and formally presented a lengthy memorandum which outlined the reasons they felt they should be granted aid and their recommendations for its use. The memo pointed out that the proposed program had been "pared to a minimum" and only amounted to approximately "1% of the current annual national budget of the United States has less than 1/10th of ERP [European Recovery Program, the Marshall Plan] requirements for the coming fiscal year." Furthermore, aid to China had proved in the past, the memo reminded its readers, to be mutually beneficial.

> In their desire to promote trade relations with the United States, the Chinese Government and people have been pleased to observe the stimulating effect of the China Aid Program upon trade between the two countries. Every bale of cotton financed by ECA under the China Aid Program was shipped by a United States exporter. Scores of United States cotton exporters were included in the Program. The petroleum program, from shipment to distribution, was largely handled by two major American oil companies. In a year of agricultural surpluses in the United States, all the wheat and flour shipped to China under the ECA Program, of which a large portion was in the form of flour processed in American mills, was from the United States. United States rice was also included in the aid program. The entire 1948-49 IEFC allocation of United States fertilizer for China was lifted through ECA. Except for some Chinese ships carrying rice from Siam and Europe to China, practically all the above-mentioned ECA commodities were shipped in United States vessels. United States banking institutions played a large part in financing the transactions connected with procurement and shipment of commodities to China. While procurement and installation under reconstruction and replacement projects have been suspended, most of the pre-project engineering have (sic) been undertaken by well-known United States engineering firms, including J.G. White Engineering Corporation which serves as the technical consultant to the Joint ECA-CUSA Committee for Reconstruction and Rehabilitation. Techni-

---

Association of China also sent an appeal for additional aid. These "lobbying" activities on the part of many Chinese citizens reported in *Chinese News Service,* December 2, 1948, December 15, 1948.

** It was to be a very active retirement for he continued to control the Nationalists and the budget, so his replacement, Li Tsung-jen, was virtually without power. Tang Tsou, *America's Failure in China, 1941-50* (2 vols.; Chicago: The University of Chicago Press, 1963), II, 497-98.

cal personnel and consulting firms from the United States have also assisted in the Rural Reconstruction programs.

The amount requested in the memorandum was $420,000,000 — $320,000,000 for commodities, and $100,000,000 for replacement and reconstruction.* [94]

In America there were three primary points of view on the issue of additional aid for the Nationalists. On February 25, 1949, Senator Pat McCarran of Nevada introduced a bill to provide $1,500,000,000 for continued assistance to China's government. His position represented the views of several members of Congress and others in the United States who felt massive aid could still turn the tide against the Communists.** The administration represented a second position and hoped to provide only the aid which had already been voted and not extend the aid bill beyond its expiration date in April, 1949. Lapham's view was between the two. Although he no longer believed the Communists could be stopped, he hoped the United States could stay in touch with whatever government came into power, and could keep America's "foot in the door." He preferred a year's extension of ECA with an appropriation of about $250,000,000 which would carry on the operation at the same level on the mainland and would also provide funds for Taiwan. [95]

At a meeting with the Secretary of State and the Chief of the Far Eastern Desk, Walton Butterworth, on March 9, Lapham discovered that when he recommended continued "commodity aid to Shanghai and Canton as long as those cities remained under non-Communist control, there was a lifting of eyebrows." [96] State did not want aid to go to the cities remaining in ECA's program beyond the time when the money which had already been appropriated was used, regardless of whether or not the cities stayed in non-Communist hands. The only

---

* It is interesting to note that rural reconstruction, which had become the favorite of American aid officials, and which was to be the only program to survive after June, 1949, was not included in the plan outlined by the Nationalists when they requested further aid from the United States in the spring.

**Many of the people who supported massive aid to China believed Asia was as important as Europe to America's national interest. According to this argument, Chiang Kai-shek deserved help because he was waging war against the Communists. China was thought to be the " 'active Theatre' in the cold war," and a "testing ground for tactics they [the Communists] might use to take over the world." *China and U.S. Far East Policy, 1945-1967* (Washington, D.C.: Congressional Quarterly Service, 1967), p. 45.

program the Department was willing to allow to continue was the JCRR which they felt could be funded out of unexpended ECA money. State was opposed to any further aid beyond this and recommended an orderly liquidation for ECA.[97]

In a letter to Senator Tom Connally, Chairman of the Senate Committee on Foreign Relations, Dean Acheson outlined the State Department's position on the proposed aid bill. According to Acheson, the "bill proposes aid of a magnitude and character unwarranted by present circumstances in China." In spite of the $2,000,000,000 which the United States had spent on aid since V-J Day, the Nationalist government had not been able to defeat the Communists militarily and had not tried to implement any of the reforms deemed necessary in the United States "to provide a basis of economic improvement and political stability." The Secretary reiterated America's desire to steer clear of further involvement in the "fratricidal" war and indicated that he felt massive aid to the Nationalists would be resented by the war-weary Chinese people as "an extreme infringement of China's sovereignty."

On the other hand, the Department felt obliged to continue to "give assistance to areas under the control of the Chinese Government which it continues to recognize." The recommendation, therefore, that State was considering was the use of the 1948 China Aid Act's unexpended funds beyond the expiration date of April 2, 1949, for a limited period of time. "If during such a period, the situation in China clarifies itself sufficiently, further recommendations might be made." [98]

Again Roger Lapham was disappointed that the State Department view differed from his own. After the March 10 meeting with Acheson and Butterworth, he wrote Allen Griffin, "I left in a very gloomy and disgusted mood." In a meeting with Hoffman the following morning, Lapham

> Told him that if State had really and finally made up its mind to abandon the mainland save for JCRR that I felt like blowing my top. However I realized Hoffman's main concern was to put over the ERP part of the program as promptly as possible and I didn't want to do anything to make things more difficult for him. Further I realized that his main job was to play ball with State and to avoid as far as possible any differences of opinion with State.* [99]

*The *China White Papers*, I, 408, says the State Department supported an ECA proposal recommending extension of the aid bill so that funds already appro-

In spite of this avowal of his sympathy for Hoffman's position, Lapham did not immediately end his efforts to obtain additional aid. Even though the State Department opposed his plan, he thought Congress might be receptive to his proposals. In a memo to Hoffman a few days after their meeting, he pointed out:

> It would appear that many Senators and Congressmen are still anxious to help China, and if ECA advanced a reasonable proposal . . . it would be welcomed in many quarters and would perhaps influence State in withdrawing from what on the surface today seems a policy which would invite further criticism . . . In closing I reiterate my strong conviction that it is not only proper but right for ECA to express its recommendations. First an attempt should be made before any recommendation is submitted to Congress to secure State approval or at least smoke out further ideas from State if it has any, but failing State approval or any compromise, ECA should submit its ideas directly to Congress.[100]

In a meeting with the Senate Foreign Relations Committee on March 24 he presented his point of view. He got the same impression from this meeting, however, that he had gotten from the meetings with State Department officials.* They were not likely to favor further aid and were willing only to extend the aid bill long enough to spend appropriated funds.[101] He received a somewhat more favorable impression from his meeting the following day with the House Foreign Affairs Committee, but, when the matter was voted on, the State Department recommendation was favored. On April 14, 1949, new legislation was written which left dispersal of the unexpended funds of the 1948 China Aid Act in the hands of the President. No additional aid money was appropriated.[102]

The Nationalists were undoubtedly disappointed that their request for $420,000,000 had been turned down. There were those in China, however, who were relieved that massive aid would not be coming from

---

priated could be spent until December, 1949. This gives a slightly different impression than one gets from Lapham's Papers and may indicate that proposals from Paul Hoffman with which the State Department concurred differed from Lapham's recommendations.

 * Lapham had had a meeting with Acheson on March 23 at which he wrote there were "just the two of us." The Secretary had said he would give "due consideration" to Lapham's remarks, but the ECA official did not feel his arguments had impressed Acheson. Memorandum to R. Allen Griffin from Roger Lapham, March 24, 1949. Lapham Papers.

the United States. On March 23, 1949, John M. Cabot, American Consul General in Shanghai, reported on a meeting to Ambassador Stuart. The meeting had been with two members of the Department League. At one time, the League had been a third political party, but had recently aligned itself with the Communists as the "lesser of two evils." In spite of their new allegiance, many League members, who had been educated in the United States, liked America and hoped to be the catalyst in establishing friendly relations between the Communists and the United States. They objected to additional aid for the Nationalists, therefore, "not only because such continued support would needlessly prolong the war and intensify Communist hatred of the United States but also because it would tend to destroy the pro-American sentiment of Democratic Leaders, who now must go along with the Communists." [103]

The Communists, meanwhile, expressed utter confidence in their invincibility. At a Communist National Congress in April, they accurately predicted that in six months to a year, they would be in control all over China and that "no help by American imperialism could avert KMT's annihilation." [104]

When Roger Lapham returned to China in April to wind up his involvement with ECA, he was astounded to find how much the situation had changed since he left in February. In a letter to Paul Hoffman on May 9, he wrote of the tremendous advances the Communists had made, their insulting treatment of Ambassador Stuart,*[105] the Nationalist evacuation of their capital at Nanking, and the move of ECA headquarters to Canton.[106] Throughout May and June, Lapham and Griffin and other ECA officials reduced the programs until only JCRR remained.

Although he had not been able to influence American policy into what he considered a more positive approach, he was a pragmatic man and he continued to hope that the United States would not be completely shut out of China.** In a letter to Juan Trippe, Chairman of the Board

---

*On the morning of April 24, the Ambassador had been awakened by Communist soldiers entering his bedroom. He accepted their explanation that they were "looking around for fun and meant no harm." It seemed to Stuart that the State Department later made more of this incident than it deserved. J. Leighton Stuart, *Fifty Years in China,* pp. 239-40.

**In a letter to Fred Eldridge, who had been a Public Relations Officer with General Joseph W. Stilwell during World War II, R. Allen Griffin expressed his opinion of the

of Pan American Airways, written shortly after Lapham returned to his home in San Francisco, he wrote a summation of his views:

1. Apparently there is nothing to stop the Communist military advance on the mainland. I believe that they can occupy Canton whenever they want to and later, the west and northwest.

2. What now appears to have been the State Department's policy right along, "Let the fires burn out and the dust settle," is the only practical course we can pursue today — whether we like it or not.

3. A possible alternative would be to send a fullsized military expedition of our own to fight the Communists on the mainland. The Congress certainly would not go for that, nor would I . . .

4. General Chennault's thought that an American-manned airforce could knock out the Communists is, to my way of thinking, just plain cockeyed . . .

5. Senator Knowland's hazy thoughts that we can dig up some unknown White Hope leader and effectively back him is just wishful thinking. If any honest, capable anti-Communist Chinese leader is to appear, he must rise first under his own power, and not be put forward by any foreigner.

6. I would not put another cent behind the Generalissimo and the Kuomintang reactionaries; and I cannot enthuse about supporting Taiwan to be used as a military springboard for a come-back on the mainland.

7. If it is necessary for our national security that Taiwan be held by a government friendly to the United States, I would go the limit to kick out

---

China Mission. "All of the conditions that thwarted Joe Stillwell (sic) during your period with him in China flourish today under the same uspicies (sic) that existed then. In fact, by and large, the same old faces preside over the decisions and the same kind of decisions result in further obfuscation of American efforts to 'do good for China.'

However, this experience is priceless, and if my associates and I have not been able to get the results we hoped for in our economic program, at least our experience has not diminished our stature as thinking human beings that have made a strenuous effort to do a job well. At least our reputations remain sound, even though the time may come when they are chasing us through the streets.

Some day when we get together I will give you the inside story of the ideas that evolved in our senior staff and the suggestions that we strenuously made to Washington. I am sure you will be much interested, as this story has not been in the news. Because our suggestions were not taken to the bosom of the State Department — appearing more as a viper to them than a hot water bottle — we feel pretty discouraged. That means that we may have gone the way of all those Americans who have come here and tried to do their damndest. However, we are still trying, although we have precious little to work with any more in the manner in which we would like to work — and the same old crowd to deal with." Letter to Fred Edlridge from R. Allen Griffin, February 18, 1949. Griffin Papers.

the Gimo and his buddies and make sure that Taiwan was developed for the benefit of the Taiwanese, and not for the Nationalist mainlanders.

8. Maybe such a course of action, if initiated in Taiwan six months ago, might have been successful; but I very much doubt whether it is the right course to pursue today.

9. If no affirmative action is possible today, and I do not believe it is, there is one thing we should not do — and that is to make it more difficult for the American businessman, the American missionary, doctor and teacher to carry on in the Chinese mainland, to the extent the Chinese Communists will allow. I would strongly oppose any effort to impose at this end, an economic blocade (sic) other than to refuse the export of munitions and strategic war materials. Let's keep the door open as far as possible and not deliberately build up an iron curtain, ourselves — thus forcing the Chinese to turn more and more to Moscow.[107]

In the near future, however, the Open Door was to be firmly closed by both the new regime in China and the United States. During Lapham's year in the country which he said he "wouldn't have missed . . . for anything," [108] American policy became more firmly anti-Communist while, on the other hand, the Truman administration refused to commit itself to an aid program for the Nationalists massive enough to change the course of the civil war.* Recommendations made by ECA leaders in the course of their mission proved to be unacceptable to policy makers in Washington. American officials were against aid to regional leaders which they felt would be ineffectual and would serve to undermine America's ally, Chiang Kai-shek. They opposed dispersal of residual aid to any areas where the supplies might fall into Communist hands. They disagreed with Lapham's suggestions for firm and unilateral action in regard to Taiwan. They refused to support a program which would give additional aid money to the almost defeated Nationalists. In each case, they chose the course of action which seemed most closely aligned with America's national interest, although, as has been noted, ECA leaders frequently held contradictory opinions on how this could best be done.

---

* There was to be a great deal of controversy in coming years about China policy at this time. Shortly after the *China White Paper* was published in August, 1949, David Gordon, of the International Bank for Reconstruction and Development, wrote Roger Lapham a terse summation of what he called the "contradictory and irresponsible . . . U.S. Government thinking on China." According to Gordon, "the reasoning of American policy makers, stripped to its essentials, seems to have been somewhat as follows:
1) The Kuomintang regime is a recognized sovereign government and must be the sole recipient of any help to China.

Chapter 7 Footnotes

[1] Memorandum by Harlan Cleveland, July, 1948. Roger D. Lapham Papers, Hoover Institution on War, Revolution and Peace, Stanford, California.

[2] Memorandum entitled "Aid to China Policy" by Harlan Cleveland, September 13, 1948. Lapham Papers.

[3] Memorandum to Paul Hoffman from Harlan Cleveland, September 19,1948. Lapham Papers.

[4] Memorandum to Paul Hoffman from Harlan Cleveland, September 1, 1948. Lapham Papers.

[5] Memorandum to Paul Hoffman from Harland Cleveland, September 19, 1948. Lapham Papers.

[6] Tang Tsou, *America's Failure in China, 1941-50*, II, 479.

[7] Memorandum to M. T. Moore from Harlan Cleveland, July 31, 1948. Lapham Papers.

[8] Memorandum to Paul Hoffman from Roger Lapham, September 27, 1948. Lapham Papers.

[9] *China White Paper*, I, 253.

[10] *Ibid.*, II, 905.

[11] *Ibid.*, PP. 907-911.

[12] *Ibid.*, pp. 872-74.

[13] C.P. Fitzgerald, *The Birth of Communist China*, p. 110.

[13a] Notes of Meetings with General Fu Tso-yi and Vice-President Li Tsung-jen, July 28, 1948, and of Meeting with Li Tsung-jen on July 31, 1948. Griffin Papers.

[14] Letter to Paul Hoffman from Roger Lapham, November 12, 1948. Lapham Papers.

[14a] Notes of Meeting with Admiral Oscar C. Badger, August 5, 1948. Griffin Papers.

[15] From Admiral Badger's testimony, *Military Situation in the Far East*, IV, 2745.

[16] Admiral Badger's letter to Secretary of Defense James V. Forrestal quoted by Badger in testimony in *Ibid.*, p. 2746.

[17] *Ibid.*, p. 2764.

[18] *China White Paper*, I, 319.

---

2)   Any effective system of supervision and control of our assistance would be an invasion of Chinese sovereignty.

3)   But the government is also hopelessly incompetent and corrupt, so any aid given would be certain to be wasted.

4)   But public pressure in the U.S., responding to the rising Soviet threat, makes some counteraction in China inescapable; the Nationalist Government is the only available channel through which such counteraction can be taken.

5)   Our assistance is sure to go down a rathole and the result will be a great scandal; to avoid getting involved in that mess we (the U.S. Government) should avoid like the plague any responsibility for the way in which our help is used.

6)   At the same time we should point out at every opportunity the sins of the Chinese Government and exhort it to hit the sawdust trail.

7)   When all this aid and these exhortations eventually prove fruitless, as they inevitably will, there will be a clear record that we warned of what would happen and had nothing to do with it; and that record can then be incorporated in a voluminous White Paper which will absolve us of all responsibility.

Letter to Roger Lapham from David Gordon, August 26, 1949. Griffin Papers.

[19] Interview with R. Allen Griffin, January 20, 1971.
[20] Memorandum to M. T. Moore from Harlan Cleveland, July 31, 1948. Lapham Papers.
[21] Memorandum to Paul Hoffman from Harlan Cleveland, September 1, 1948. Lapham Papers.
[22] Report of the Army briefing to Roger Lapham from Paul Hoffman, October 2, 1948. Lapham Papers.
[23] Telephone call reported in a letter to M. T. Moore from Charles L. Stillman, October 9, 1948. Lapham Papers.
[24] Cable to Roger Lapham from Paul Hoffman, October 1, 1948. Lapham Papers.
[25] Cable to Paul Hoffman from Roger Lapham, October 5, 1948. Lapham Papers.
[26] Letter to Major General A. R. Bolling from Allen Griffin, October 9, 1948. Lapham Papers.
[27] Letter to M. T. Moore from Charles L. Stillman, October 8, 1948. Lapham Papers.
[28] Memorandum to Paul Hoffman from Charles L. Stillman, October 9, 1948. Lapham Papers.
[29] Memorandum from James Grant to Roger Lapham, October 9, 1948. Memorandum from John D. Sumner to Roger Lapham, October 9, 1948. Lapham Papers.
[30] Memorandum by Harlan Cleveland entitled "Notes on Military Aid for China," October 9, 1948. Lapham Papers.
[31] D. Worth Clark Report, n.d. Hornbeck Papers.
[32] Statement submitted by Bridgadier General T. S. Timberman to the Committee on Foreign Affairs of the House of Representatives, June 21, 1949. *China White Paper,* II, 975-980.
[33] Colonel W. Bruce Pirnie, USAF, Res., "Who Hamstrings U.S. Military Aid to China?," *China Monthly,* (October, 1948), 288-291.
[34] Letter to R. Allen Griffin from Roger Lapham, October 25, 1948. Lapham Papers.
[35] *Ibid.*
[36] *Ibid.*
[37] *New York Times,* October 19,1948.
[38] Letter to R. Allen Griffin from Roger Lapham, October 25, 1948. Lapham Papers.
[39] Conversation with Admiral Badger reported to Harlan Cleveland by R. Allen Griffin, November 8, 1948. Lapham Papers.
[40] Conference with Ambassador Stuart reported in *Ibid.*
[41] *China White Paper,* II, 975-980.
[42] C.P. Fitzgerald, *The Birth of Communist China,* pp. 113-14.
[43] *Ibid.*
[44] Memorandum to Harlan Cleveland from R. Allen Griffin, November, 1948. Griffin Papers.
[45] Cable to Secretary of State, Washington, D.C. and U.S. Embassy, Nanking, and to Paul Hoffman, November 26, 1948. Lapham Papers.
[46] Harlan Cleveland to Roger Lapham, December 1, 1948. Lapham Papers.
[47] Harlan Cleveland to Roger Lapham, December 2, 1948. Lapham Papers.
[48] *Ibid.*
[49] Walter Millis (ed.), *The Forrestal Diaries,* p. 517.
[50] *Ibid.,* pp. 532-33.
[51] *Ibid.,* p. 533.
[52] Memorandum to Paul Hoffman from Roger Lapham, December 11, 1948. Lapham Papers.
[53] *Ibid.*
[54] Schedule of Paul Hoffman's activities in China, December 11-15, 1948. Griffin Papers.

124   The Marshall Plan for China

55 Transcript of Paul Hoffman's Press Conference, Shanghai, China, December 13, 1948. Griffin Papers.

56 Copy of the agreement dated December 14, 1948. Lapham Papers.

57 Letter to Paul Hoffman from Roger Lapham in which he mentions he is delighted that Hoffman agrees with his suggestions, December 16, 1948. Lapham Papers.

58 Harlan Cleveland from Roger Lapham, December 22, 1948. Lapham Papers.

59 *New York Times*, December 19, 1948.

60 *Ibid.*, December 22, 1948.

61 *Ibid.*

62 Memorandum to Roger Lapham from Harlan Cleveland, January 6, 1949. Lapham Papers.

63 Memorandum to Roger Lapham from Harlan Cleveland, January 7, 1949. Lapham Papers.

64 *Ibid.*

65 Cabinet meeting and President's decision reported to Roger Lapham by Harlan Cleveland, January 15 and January 21, 1949. Lapham Papers.

66 Letter to Roger Lapham from R. Allen Griffin from Washington, D. C., January 18, 1949. Lapham Papers.

67 J. Leighton Stuart, *Fifty Years in China*, p. 220.

68 *Chinese News Service*, February 11, 1949. Mao Tse-tung's article from the Cominform magazine published in Bucharest, Rumania, and quoted in a Communist broadcast on November 7, 1949.

69 *Ibid.* Liu Shao-chi's article entitled "On Internationalism and Nationalism" from the *China Digest*, December 14, 1948.

70 United States Economic Cooperation Administration, Mission to China, Tientsin Regional Office, *General Situation Report of Tientsin* for February 1 - March 19, 1949. Griffin Papers.

71 *Ibid.*

72 Joseph W. Ballantine, *Formosa: A Problem for United States Foreign Policy* (Washington, D.C.: The Brookings Institution, 1952), pp. 116-140.

73 Thomas E. Dewey, *Journey to the Far Pacific*, p. 308.

74 Interview with General Douglas MacArthur, January 30, 1949. Lapham Papers.

75 Memorandum on policy for Taiwan to Secretary of State Dean Acheson and the American Embassay, Nanking, from Roger Lapham. Lapham Papers.

76 *New York Times*, February 9, 1949.

77 Cable to Roger Lapham from Paul Hoffman, February 11, 1949. Lapham Papers.

78 *New York Times*, February 18, 1949. Another source says, "Substantial ECA operations in Formosa began in January, 1949." Joseph W. Ballantin, *Formosa*, p. 134.

79 Letter to Roger Lapham from R. Allen Griffin, February 25, 1949. Lapham Papers.

80 Memorandum to Paul Hoffman from Roger Lapham, February 15, 1949. Lapham Papers.

81 *Ibid.*, March 9, 1949. Lapham Papers.

82 Memorandum to Roger Lapham from R. Allen Griffin, March 19, 1949. Lapham Papers.

83 Memorandum to Harlan Cleveland from R. Allen Griffin, May 11, 1949. Griffin Papers.

84 Cable to Secretary of State Dean Acheson form R. Allen Griffin, June 1, 1949. Griffin Papers.

85 Memorandum to Paul Hoffman from Harlan Cleveland, March 1, 1949. Lapham Papers.

[86] Memorandum to R. Allen Griffin from Roger Lapham, March 17, 1949. Lapham Papers.

[87] *Ibid.*, March 22, 1949. Lapham Papers.

[88] Memorandum prepared for Ambassador-at-Large Philip C. Jessup by Roger Lapham and R. Allen Griffin, September 10, 1949. Griffin Papers.

[89] Letter to H. Medill Sarkisian from Roger Lapham, January 27, 1950. Griffin Papers.

[90] *China White Paper,* II, 888-89.

[91] *China and U.S. Far East Policy, 1945-1967* (Washington, D.C.: Congressional Quarterly Service, 1967), p. 45.

[92] Walter Millis (ed.), *The Forrestal Diaries,* p. 533.

[93] Memorandum to Paul Hoffman from Roger Lapham, November 29, 1948. Lapham Papers.

[94] *Memorandum on Continuation of United States Aid to China, 1949.* Griffin Papers.

[95] Memorandum to Paul Hoffman from Roger Lapham, March 14, 1949. Lapham Papers.

[96] Letter to R. Allen Griffin from Roger Lapham, March 17, 1949. Lapham Papers.

[97] Memorandum to Paul Hoffman from Roger Lapham, March 14, 1949. Lapham Papers.

[98] Letter to Senator Tom Connally from Secretary of State Dean Acheson, March 15, 1949. *China White Paper,* II, 1053-54.

[99] Letter to R. Allen Griffin from Roger Lapham, March 17, 1949. Lapham Papers.

[100] Memorandum to Paul Hoffman from Roger Lapham, March 17, 1949. Lapham Papers.

[101] Memorandum to R. Allen Griffin from Roger Lapham, March 24, 1949. Lapham Papers.

[102] *China White Paper.* I, 408-409.

[103] Report to Ambassador Stuart from John M. Cabot, American Consul General in Shanghai, March 23, 1949, on a conversation Cabot had with two members of the Democratic League.

[104] Report to the American Consulate in Shanghai from Consul O. Edmund Clubb, Peking, April 14, 1949, on the Communist National Congress, April 11, 1949.

[105] J. Leighton Stuart, *Fifty Years in China,* pp. 239-40.

[106] Letter to Paul Hoffman from Roger Lapham, May 9, 1949. Lapham Papers.

[107] Letter to Mr. Juan T. Trippe, Chairman of the Board, Pan American World Airways, July 7, 1949. Griffin Papers.

[108] *Ibid.*

MAP III
JCRR OFFICES AND SOME PROJECT AREAS
Regional Offices Underlined

Conclusions

America's China policy in the year ECA operated on the mainland was molded by traditional empathy for China, the dream of the millions of potential customers, and the desire for a stable ally in Asia. All of these factors were shaped in the postwar world by the growth of the power of the Soviet Union and the assumption on the part of American policy makers that the Russians were carrying out a world plan which included control of China.

During the ECA mission, two men were primarily responsible for America's policy — President Harry S. Truman and Secretary of State George C. Marshall. Truman believed in exercising his Constitutional rights on foreign policy. In his *Memoirs,* he stated his feelings on this subject:

> The official position of the United States . . . is defined by the decisions and declarations of the President. There can be only one voice in stating the position of this country in the field of foreign relations.[1]

He considered the Secretary of State the most important Cabinet member and expected to be kept fully informed by him. The decisions, however, he intended to make alone. His relationships with both George Marshall and Dean Acheson were exceptionally congenial and productive.

At the time of the aid mission, the President's decisions were influenced by Marshall's views of policy needs and priorities, the most important tenet of which was a Europe-first concept. It seemed to the Secretary that aid to Europe would be much more effectively used than aid to China, an opinion which was undoubtedly strengthened by his experience on the Marshall Mission. He had little faith in Chiang Kai-shek who had not followed his military advice nor instituted the multitude of governmental reforms Marshall thought China needed. An adept military strategist, he knew that the only American commitment likely to succeed was massive military support, and he was as devoted to the notion that this should not happen as he correctly judged the American public to be. He did not want the United States to

127

become more involved in China's civil war. In fact, he probably would have liked to withdraw from China completely and let the situation resolve itself. Faced with political pressure in the United States, however, he concluded that the administration had to make a token effort, but when he referred to the aid program of 1948 as a "stay of execution," he revealed that in his own opinion this was only a half-hearted effort.

Because of their need to maintain a world view of American relations abroad, the President and Secretary of State controlled policy and their attitudes were influenced very little by men on government assignment in China. As often happened, people in the field became overly concerned with the country to which they were assigned. In spite of their greater understanding of what was happening in their areas, they sometimes made policy suggestions which did not fit in with Washington's perspective. As W. Walton Butterworth correctly pointed out, extensive plans made in the field were not of great importance because the ultimate decisions had to be made in Washington.[2] This proved to be a constant source of irritation and frustration to American representatives in China.*

Although both the President and Secretary of State spoke highly of Ambassador J. Leighton Stuart, his suggestions were rarely acted on. Stuart knew that his ideas were not highly regarded by the State Department. In the summer of 1948, he had received specific cabled instructions to report only the facts of the situation in China and to eliminate his advice on United States policies. He told mission leaders that "while the cable was not worded this bluntly, it was made plain to me that Washington did not desire to be advised to change the kind of policy it had."[2a] Stuart, however, continued to believe in the opinion he expressed to General Marshall in 1947: the United States should give the Nationalists enough help to defeat the Communists or should get out of China's affairs completely.** Stuart later wrote that:

* Historian Barbara W. Tuchman noted the comments of two representatives in the field on this subject. "Willys Peck, Counselor of the Nanking Embassy in 1936, wrote of 'the bottom of the void into which (we sometimes feel) we drop our reports to Washington.' The Consul in Yunnan, A. R. Ringwalt, voiced the same complaint, "Especially in an outpost like this one gets the feeling that one is merely writing for one's own amusement, and that reports when received are merely filed away without any notice having been taken of their content.' " Barbara W. Tuchman, *Stilwell and the American Experience in China, 1911-1945* (New York: The Macmillian Company, 1970), pp. 204-205n.

** John F. Melby was assigned to the American Embassy in China from 1945 to 1949. During that time he recorded many comments about Ambassador Stuart in his diary. In

Either would have been better than a hesitating, half-hearted form of continuing assistance. I had long been observing the unfortunate results of this third course and had myself become a helpless target for the vicious anti-American denunciation this had provoked.[3]

Admiral Oscar C. Badger also felt the need for better communication with leaders in Washington. He said in later testimony he had never been able to find out why the aid he had recommended for Fu Tso-yi, which had been approved by the Joint Chiefs of Staff, had arrived late and in poor condition.[4] He considered himself the leading military commander in China and felt he had been overruled in a way which was not satisfactorily explained.

Roger Lapham's policy suggestions were not met with approbation either. Usually his ideas were conveyed to Harlan Cleveland and/or Paul Hoffman and although the ECA officials in Washington often approved recommendations from the China mission, the State Department had more power and more influence with the President.

---

his book, wherein he incorporated portions of his diary, he noted, "During the next three years [after Stuart's appointment as Ambassador] those of us who had had reservations came to have great respect for his ability and deep affection for him as a human being. I think what affected us most was the growing realization that he so passionately loved the Chinese people and was so heartsick over what was happening to them that he would do literally anything that gave any kind of hope of stopping the slaughter to which they were still being subjected. Nothing else moved him, not even the august Department of State, whose instructions he on occasion did not bother to read." p. 137. On October 28, 1948, Melby recorded in his Diary, "Meanwhile the State *prototypes for successful programs on Taiwan.* On the negative side, the Department tells Dr. Stuart to inform the Generalissimo any advice he is giving is personal and without the approval of the United States Government. Increasingly the evidence is that he is up to his ears dickering in internal Chinese politics. I am morally certain he is actively working day and night on a coalition." p. 288. If Stuart was still working on a coalition government, he was doing so after Washington had long since given up any hope for a peaceful compromise between the Nationalists and the Communists. For further comments on the Ambassador by Melby, see John F. Melby, *The Mandate of Heaven,* pp. 134-38, 181-82, 264-65, 274-77, 287-88. In an interview with General Douglas MacArthur, the relationship between Ambassador Stuart and the State Department was discussed by the General and Roger Lapham. Lapham apparently gave MacArthur some information he had not had before and to which he replied: "Until you told me this minute that Ambassador Stuart had been instructed not to submit any more policy recommendations to the State Department, I could not have believed that any diplomatic representative of the United States Government could be so restricted. I am very seldom shocked to the extent of having my breath taken away, but what you say about Ambassador Stuart . . . takes my breath away. It is inconceivable that an accredited Ambassador of the United States Government should ever be placed in so humiliating a position." Interview with General Douglas MacArthur, January 30, 1949. Lapham Papers.

ECA leaders, then, had little effect on overall policy. The aid program they ran, however, had some immediate results. The commodities fed starving people and provided jobs by supplying raw materials to factories, and the rural and industrial reconstruction programs provided additional propaganda for Communist charges that America had taken over Japan's imperialistic aims in Asia. The mission also helped alienate a formerly pro-American group of Chinese. C. Y. W. Meng, in an article in *The China Weekly Review* in March, 1949, said he was accepting ECA rice reluctantly and with many reservations since he was not sure American aid was helping his country. He said there were many people in China who did not want the United States to continue its aid program.* "Mr. Lapham's proposal for new aid to 'Nationalist' China was greeted with a quick and unamimous 'unwanted' by Chinese professors, editors, liberals, peace-sponsors, and even by some legislators." This he attributed primarily to "the injection of military overtones into a program which was supposed to be purely economic," and the fact that American leadership was overridden with "the 'excessive' American fear of totalitarianism and mass red hysteria."[5] The disaffection of this group of Chinese was unfortunate and was probably the most devasting effect of the aid program for, as Dr. Dorothy Borg pointed out, although good will is not the most vital aspect of foreign affairs, it does play a part, and recent American policy had done more to lose good will than gain it.[6]

As for other profound effects on the affairs of China, it is difficult to see that ECA made significant changes. The economic part of the program was so minute when projected on the needs of the population that it can be said to have had little lasting influence. The military part of the China Aid Act did not change the course of the war in favor of the Nationalists. The grant itself of $125,000,000 was not enough to

---

* Mao Tse-tung cited an example of a man who earlier had been willing to die rather than accept American aid. "Chu Tse-ching (1898-1948), Chinese man of letters and university professor. After the War of Resistance, he actively supported the student movement against the Chiang Kai-shek regime. In June 1948 he signed a declaration protesting against the revival of Japanese militarism, which was being fostered by the United States, and rejecting 'U.S. relief' flour. He was then living in great poverty. He died in Peiping on August 12, 1948 from poverty and illness, but even on his death-bed he enjoined his family not to buy the U.S. flour rationed by the Kuomintang government." Mao Tse-tung, *Selected Works 1945-49* (5 vols., New York: International Publishers, 1954), V, 440.

accomplish this and, of the allotted amount, a little less than half was actually spent for military aid for the mainland.[7]

As Roger Lapham later concluded in a letter to a friend,

> Somehow or another, I don't believe anything we did do or failed to do would have had material effect. It seems to me that there has been a real revolution going on in Asia for some years past, and that it is still going on — an awakening of so-called backward people — a rising urge to run their own show — an up-surge of resentment against the way they have been treated by the Western powers in the past. Maybe something too big for you and I to comprehend.[8]

The tragedy, of course, was not that Roger Lapham may not have comprehended, but the American policy makers failed to. Or if they comprehended it, their actions were controlled by the conviction that the upsurge of nationalism and revolution carried a "Made in Moscow" sign. This Cold War conviction, which was to grow during the aid mission's year in China, helped bring about several important changes in America's role in international relations, the ramifications of which have been felt ever since.

As the power struggle with Russia intensified, the need for military preparedness grew, and America made a series of military liaisons. The first peacetime alliance was the North Atlantic Treaty Organization (NATO) in 1949, and was followed by many others as adjuncts of policy. The China aid mission represented one of the early programs which were characterized by the growing association of military and economic aid.

When it became obvious that the two major Cold War powers were deadlocked, the art of diplomacy, as a means of keeping the lines of communication open between countries, diminished in importance. It may even be argued that America's traditional notion of war as an aberration representing a breakdown in policy had been replaced by the Clausewitzian concept of war as continuation of policy. This seems particularly feasible in both the Korean and Vietnamese wars which were extensions of America's anti-communist crusade.[9]

A further result of the constant focus on the world power struggle was the enhanced power of the President. As Senator Arthur Vandenberg noted:

> The trouble is that these "crises" never reach Congress until they have developed to a point where Congressional discretion is pathetically re-

stricted. When things finally reach a point where a President asks us to "declare war" there usually is nothing left except to "declare war." [10]

The complaint continues to be heard and the solution has not yet been found. The powers of the President increased as the powers of Congress to do anything to control the Executive diminished. The China aid program provided one small example of the early beginnings of the increased importance of the President's role. The unexpended funds of the military portion of the aid bill were voted to be dispersed at the President's discretion. Congress, which had appropriated the funds, voted that their expenditure be placed in the hands of the Executive. During the Viet Nam War, the suggestion was made that Congress withhold appropriations but no vote was able to curb the President's powers in this way.

Another adjunct of the Cold War, which was to have far-reaching consequences and which was implicit in the China Aid act, centered on giving support to governments as long as they could be judged to be on "our side." America's rhetorical goal for helping countries toward social change became secondary to the predominant aim of stopping communism. The position the United States had enjoyed as the leading example and proponent of colonial revolt was compromised by support of status quo leaders. Aid to Chiang Kai-shek marked one of the early examples of this.

All of these Cold War policies, which were to change America's traditional role in international relations, were nascent in the aid mission. In spite of this, China policy became the center of an attack on the Truman administration which was one of the most vindictive in American history. After the Nationalists lost, every aspect of earlier China policy was minutely scrutinized for signs that it was part of a communist conspiracy within the United States government. ECA officials were not singled out for abuse, but the program was said to have been too little and too late.

The years have diminished both the harshness of the criticism and the inflexibility of Cold War policies. There is even renewed hope that one day a rapprochement may be reached between Communist China and the United States. As for the China aid mission, its last ditch effort to maintain the status quo was destined to fail. No outside power could bolster the faltering Nationalists nor provide them with the internal impulse they needed to retain their leadership in China. When Roger

Lapham wrote, "I don't believe anything we did do or failed to do would have had material effect," he was expressing considerably more than a rationale for the mission's weaknesses. He had come to the profound realization that there were finite limits to American power, and that China would implacably mold her own destiny.

Chapter 8 Footnotes

[1] Harry S. Truman, *Memoirs,* II, 405.

[2] Memorandum to Paul Hoffman from Harlan Cleveland, September 19, 1948. Lapham Papers.

[2a] Notes of Meeting with Ambassador J. Leighton Stuart, October 9, 1948. Griffin Papers.

[3] J. Leighton Stuart, *Fifty Years in China,* p. 244.

[4] *Military Situation in the Far East,* wherein Admiral Badger described the condition of the aid shipment and his efforts to find out why it was late, IV, 2747-48.

[5] C. Y. W. Meng, "A Chinese View of American Aid," *The China Weekly Review,* CXIII (March 19, 1949), 59.

[6] Dorothy Borg, "America Loses Chinese Good Will," *Far Eastern Survey,* XVIII (February 23, 1949), 45.

[7] *China White Paper,* II, 953.

[8] Letter to H. Medill Sarkisian from Roger Lapham, January 23, 1950. Copy in Griffin Papers.

[9] Barbara W. Tuchman, *Stilwell and the American Experience in China, 1911-45* (New York: The Macmillan Company, 1970), p. 341.

[10] Arthur H. Vandenberg, Jr. (ed.), *The Private Papers of Senator Vandenberg* (Boston: Houghton Mifflin Company, 1952), p. 342.

BIBLIOGRAPHY

MANUSCRIPTS

R. Allen Griffin Papers. In possession of owner, Monterey, California.
Stanley K. Hornbeck Papers. Archives, Hoover Institution on War, Revolution
and Peace, Stanford University, Stanford, California.
Roger D. Lapham Papers. Archives, Hoover Institution on War, Revolution
and Peace, Stanford University, Stanford, California.

GOVERNMENT DOCUMENTS
UNITED STATED DOCUMENTS

China and U.S. Far East Policy, 1945-1967. Washington, D. C.: Congressional
Quarterly Service, 1967.
Congress. Senate. Hearings before the Committee on Armed Services and the
Committee on Foreign Relations. 82nd Congress, 1st session. *Military
Situation in the Far East.* 5 vols. Washington, D. C.: 1951.
Congress. Senate. Report of the Joint Committee on Foreign Economic Coop-
eration, *China,* 80th Congress, 2d sess. Washington, December 3, 1948.

Congressional Record, 80th Congress, 2d session. Washington, D. C.: 1948.
Department of State. Publication 3573, Far Eastern Series 30. *The China White
Paper,* August, 1949. 2 vols. Stanford, California: Stanford University
Press, 1967. Originally issued as: *United States Relations With China, With
Special Reference to the Period, 1944-1949.*

ALMANACS, HANDBOOKS, AND ENCYCLOPEDIAS

Current Biography, Who's News and Why, 1948, 1949, 1951, 1961. New York: The
H. W. Wilson Company, 1949, 1950, 1952, 1962.
Kieran, John, ed. *Information Please Almanac, 1948.* New York: Doubleday &
Company, Inc., and Garden City Publishing Co., Inc., 1948.

NEWSPAPERS

New York Times, January, 1948, to July, 1949.

PERIODICALS AND MAGAZINES

Bernal, Martin. "Was Chinese Communism Inevitable?," *The New York Review
of Books,* XV (December 3, 1970), 43-47.
Borg, Dorothy. "America Loses Chinese Good Will," *Far Eastern Survey,* XVIII
(February 23, 1949), 37-45.
_____ . "ECA and US Policy in China," *Far Eastern Survey,* XVIII
(August 24, 1949), 197-200.
Chinese News Service. Pacific Coast Bureau. June 8, 1948, June 18, 1948, June

23, 1948, September 1, 1948, December 2, 1948, December 14, 1948, February 11, 1949.

Cleveland, Harlan. "Economic Aid To China," *Far Eastern Survey*, XVIII (January 12, 1949), 1-6.

Conant, Melvin, Jr. "JCRR: An Object Lesson," *Far Eastern Survey*, XX (May 2, 1951), 88-92.

Meng, C. Y. W. "A Chinese View of American Aid," *The China Weekly Review*, CXIII (March 19, 1949), 59-60.

The Nation. CLXVI (February 7, 1948), 155.

Pirnie, Colonel W. Bruce, USAF, Res. "Who Hamstrings U.S. Military Aid to China?," *China Monthly*, (October, 1948) 288-291.

"Public Opinion Polls on China," *Far Eastern Survey*, XIX (July 12, 1950), 130-131.

Schlesinger, Arthur, Jr. "Origins of the Cold War," *Foreign Affairs*, XLVI (October, 1967), 22-52.

Swope, Gerard, and Walsh, Richard J. "Mass Education Movement and JCRR," *Far Eastern Survey*, XX (July 25, 1951), 145-48.

U.S. News & World Report, April 16, 1948, p. 41. November 15, 1971, p. 21.

Walton, William. "Heavy Load for Hoffman," *The New Republic*, April 19, 1948, p. 12.

Wertenbaker, C. "The China Lobby," *The Reporter*, VI (April, 15, 1952), 4-24.

COLLECTED DOCUMENTS, LETTERS, AND WORKS

Bernstein, Barton, and Matusow, Allen J., eds. *The Truman Administration: A Documentary History*. New York & London: Harper & Row, 1966.

Mao Tse-tung. *Selected Works.* 5 vols. New York: International Pub., 1954.

DIARIES

Bodde, Derk. *Peking Diary, 1948-49, A Year of Revolution*. Greenwich, Connecticut: A Fawcett Premier Book, 1950.

Millis, Walter, ed. *The Forrestal Diaries*. New York: The Viking Press, 1951.

REMINISCENCES AND AUTOBIOGRAPHIES

Acheson, Dean. *Present at the Creation, My Years in the State Department*. New York: W. W. Norton & Company, Inc., 1969.

Beal, John Robinson. *Marshall in China*. Toronto: Doubleday & Company, Inc., 1970.

Byrnes, James F. *Speaking Frankly*. New York and London: Harper & Brothers, Publishers, 1947.

Connally, Senator Tom, as told to Steinberg, Alfred. *My Name Is Tom Connally*. New York: Thomas Y. Crowell Company, 1954.

Dewey, Thomas E. *Journey to the Far Pacific*. New York: Doubleday, 1952.

Leahy, William D. *I Was There: The Personal Story of the Chief of Staff to Presidents Roosevelt and Truman Based on His Notes and Diaries Made At the Time*. New York: Whittlesey House, McGraw-Hill Book Company, Inc., 1950.

Marshall, Katherine Tupper. *Together; Annals of an Army Wife.* New York and
    Atlanta; Tupper and Love, 1946.
Melby, John F. *The Mandate of Heaven; Record of a Civil War, China, 1945-49.*
    Toronto, Canada: University of Toronto Press, 1968.
Stuart, John Leighton. *Fifty Years in China; The Memoirs of John Leighton Stuart,
    Missionary and Ambassador.* New York; Random House, 1954.
Truman, Harry S. *Memoirs,* Vol. I, *Year of Decisions.* New York; Doubleday &
    Company, Inc., 1955. Vol. II, *Years of Trial and Hope.* New York Double-
    day & Company, Inc., 1956.
Vandenberg, Arthur H., Jr., ed. *The Private Papers of Senator Vandenberg.*
    Boston; Houghton Mifflin Company, 1952.
Wedemeyer, General Albert C. *Wedemeyer Reports.* New York; Henry Holt &
    Company, 1958.
Wilson, Rose Paige. *Marshall Remembered.* Englewood Cliffs, New Jersey;
    Prentice-Hall, 1968.

BIOGRAPHIES

Payne, Robert. *The Marshall Story; A Biography of General George C. Marshall.*
    New York; Prentice-Hall, Inc., 1951.
Phillips, Cabell. *The Truman Presidency, The History of a Triumphant Succession.*
    New York; The Macmillan Co., 1966.
Schram, Stuart. *Mao Tse-tung.* Baltimore, Maryland; Penguin Books, 1966.

MONOGRAPHS AND SPECIAL STUDIES

Kilgroe, Louisa M. "American Far Eastern Policy and the Sino-Japanese Crisis,
    1937." Unpublished master's thesis, San Jose State College, 1971.

GENERAL WORKS

Agar, Herbert. *The Price of Power, America Since 1945.* Chicago: The University
    of Chicago Press, 1957.
Ballantine, Joseph W. *Formosa: A Problem for United States Foreign Policy.*
    Washington, D. C.: The Brookings Institution, 1952.
Bohlen, Charles E. *The Transformation of American Foreign Policy.* New York : W.
    W. Norton & Company, Inc., 1969.
Borg, Dorothy. *The United States and the Far Eastern Crisis of 1933-1938 from the
    Manchurian Incident Through the Initial Stage of the Undeclared Sino-Japanese
    War.* Cambridge, Massachusetts: Harvard University Press, 1964.
Buck, Pearl. *The Exile.* New York: Reynal & Hitchcock, 1936.
Buss, Claude A. *Asia in the Modern World.* New York: Macmillan, 1964.
————————— .*The People's Republic of China.* New York: D. Van Nostrand
    Company, Inc., 1962.
Chang Kia-ngau. *The Inflationary Spiral: The Experience in China, 1939-1950.*
    Cambridge, Massachusetts: The Technology Press of Massachusetts In-
    stitute of Technology and New York: John Wiley & Sons, 1958.
Chassin, Lionel Max. *The Communist Conquest of China: A History of the Civil War,
    1945-1949.* Cambridge, Massachusetts: Harvard University Press, 1965.

Chen Po-ta. *Mao Tse-tung on the Chinese Revolution.* Peking: Foreign Languages Press, 1953.

Chinese Liberated Areas Relief Association, Information Department. *UNRRA Relief for the Chinese People.* Shanghai, July, 1947.

Chiu, S. M. *Chinese Communist Revolutionary Strategy, 1945-1949.* Princeton University: Center of International Studies, 1961.

Clubb, O. Edmund. *Twentieth Century China.* New York: Columbia University Press, 1964.

Dahl, Robert A. *Congress and Foreign Policy.* New York: W. W. Norton & Company, Inc., 1950.

DeRivera, Joseph. *The Psychological Dimension of Foreign Policy.* Columbus, Ohio: Charles E. Merrill Publishing Company, 1968.

Dulles, John Foster. *War or Peace.* New York: The Macmillan Company, 1950.

Fairbank, John King. *The United States and China.* Cambridge, Massachusetts: Harvard University Press, 1961.

Feis, Herbert. *The China Tangle: The American Effort in China from Pearl Harbor to the Marshall Mission.* New York; Atheneum, 1965.

——————. *From Trust to Terror: The Onset of the Cold War, 1945-1950.* New York: W. W. Norton & Company, Inc., 1970.

Fitzgerald, C. P. *The Birth of Communist China.* Baltimore, Maryland: Penguin Books, 1964.

Goldman, Eric F. *The Crucial Decade – And After, America, 1945-1960.* New York: Vintage Books, 1960.

Graebner, Norman A., ed. *An Uncertain Tradition: American Secretaries of State in The Twentieth Century.* New York: McGraw-Hill Book Co., 1961. 1961.

Griswold, A. Whitney. *The Far Eastern Policy of the United States.* New Haven: Yale University Press, 1938.

Horowitz, David, ed. *Containment and Revolution.* Boston: Beacon Press, 1967.

Kennan, George F. *American Diplomacy, 1900-1950.* New York: A Mentor Book, 1951.

Koen, Ross Y. *The China Lobby in American Politics.* New York: The Macmillan Company, 1960.

Lafeber, Walter. *America, Russia, and the Cold War, 1945-1966.* New York: John Wiley and Sons, Inc., 1967.

Latourette, Kenneth Scott. *The American Record in the Far East, 1945-1951.* New York: The Macmillan Company, 1953.

Montgomery, John D.; Hughes, Rufus B.; and Davis, Raymond H. *Rural Improvement and Political Development: The JCRR Model,* Washington, Comparative Administration Group, American Society for Public Administration, 1966.

Moorad, George. *Lost Peace in China.* New York: E. P. Dutton & Co., 1949.

Pelissier, Roger. *The Awakening of China, 1793-1949.* London: Secker and Warburg, 1963.

Price, Harry Bayard. *The Marshall Plan and Its Meaning.* Ithaca, New York: Cornell University Press, 1955.

Reischauer, Edwin O. *Beyond Vietnam: The United States and Asia.* New York: Vintage Books, 1967.

_____ . *Wanted: An Asia Policy.* New York: Alfred A. Knopf, 1955.

Robinson, Edgar E.; DeConde, Alexander; O'Connor, Raymond G.; and Travis, Martin B., Jr. *Powers of the President in Foreign Affairs, 1945-1965.* San Francisco: The Commonwealth Club of California (Printed by Lederer, Street & Zens Co.), 1966.

Rubin, Jacob A. *Your Hundred Billion Dollars: The Complete Story of American Foreign Aid.* Philadelphia: Chilton Books, 1964.

Russell, Bertrand. *The Problem of China.* London: Allen & Unwin, Ltd., 1922.

Schurman, Franz and Schell, Orville. *Republican China, Nationalism, War, and the Rise of Communism, 1911-1949.* New York: Vintage Books, 1967.

Spanier, John W. *American Foreign Policy Since World War II.* New York: Frederick A. Praeger, Publishers, 1968.

Tang Tsou, *America's Failure in China, 1941-50.* 2 vols. Chicago: The University of Chicago Press, 1963.

Tuchman, Barbara W. *Stilwell and the American Experience in China, 1911-45.* New York: The Macmillan Company, 1970.

Varg, Paul A. *Missionaries, Chinese, and Diplomats: The American Protestant Missionary Movement in China, 1890-1952.* Princeton, New Jersey: Princeton University Press, 1958.

Vinacke, Harold M. *Far Eastern Politics in the Postwar Period.* New York: Appleton-Century-Crofts, Inc., 1956.

Westerfield, H. Bradford. *Foreign Policy and Party Politics.* New Haven, Connecticut: Yale University Press, 1955.

Wheeler, Gerald E. *Prelude to Pearl Harbor: The United States Navy and the Far East, 1921-1931.* Columbia: University of Missouri Press, 1963.

White, Theodore H. *China: The Roots of Madness.* New York: Bantam, 1968.

_____ , and Jacoby, Annalee. *Thunger Out of China.* New York: William Sloane Associates, Inc., 1946.

Williams, William Appleman. *The Tragedy of American Diplomacy.* New York: A Delta Book, 1959.

Woodbridge, George. *UNRRA, The History of the United Nations Relief and Rehabilitation Administration.* 3 vols. New York: Columbia University Press, 1950.

Young, Arthur N. *China and the Helping Hand, 1937-1945.* Cambridge, Massachusetts: Harvard University Press, 1963.

TELEVISION

"Christian Anti-Communism Crusade: Orange County Seminar," KNEW-TV telecast, April 19, 1970. Narrator, Dr. Fred C. Schwarz. Principal speaker, Dr. Walter H. Judd.

INTERVIEWS

Interviews with R. Allen Griffin, January 20, 1971, and September 22, 1971. Monterey, California.